HOW TO BE THE BEST SUNDAY SCHOOL TEACHER YOU CAN BE

TERRY HALL

MOODY PRESS
CHICAGO

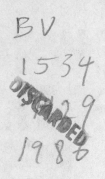

© 1986 by
THE MOODY BIBLE INSTITUTE
OF CHICAGO

All rights reserved.

The use of selected references from various versions of the Bible in this publication does not necessarily imply publisher endorsement of the versions in their entirety.

Artwork is by Bill Hovey Visuals.

Library of Congress Cataloging in Publication Data

Hall, Terry, 1941-
    How to be the best Sunday school teacher you can be.

    Includes index.
    1. Christian education—Teaching methods.   2. Sunday-school teachers.   I. Title.
BV1534.H29   1986   268'.3   86-11345
ISBN 0-8024-3631-5 (pbk.)

1 2 3 4 5 6 7 Printing/LC/Year 91 90 89 88 87 86

Printed in the United States of America

To
my mentor
Dr. Howard G. Hendricks,
master teacher and motivator

Contents

Preface

This book is for anyone who teaches the Word of God to others: pastors, Sunday school teachers, youth group workers, home Bible study leaders, and parents.

I've not always been a creative teacher, nor have I arrived where I want to be. But I'm enjoying the transition process.

When I didn't sense students experiencing joy from my ministry of the Word, I discovered Proverbs 15:2b (TLB*), "A wise teacher makes learning a joy." As I made this my regular fervent prayer, God used many influences to help make it happen.

This book is a tribute to countless students and teachers who have stimulated me to use variety and creativity. Many of their examples are sprinkled throughout these pages.

The same Holy Spirit who inspired the Word of God will illumine you as to how to apply the many ideas that follow.

Ask God daily to make you a wise teacher who makes learning a joy, and I know He will help you to be the best Sunday school teacher you can be.

*The Living Bible.

1

Preparation: Developing as a Teacher

"Don't put live eggs under a dead hen!"

That's sound advice for teachers as well as farmers. Because we can't impart what we don't possess, being the best Sunday school teacher requires personal preparation. Before teaching, we should look in four directions: up, down, in, and out.

Look Up to the Lord

Spiritual preparation for teaching starts with receiving new life in Christ. We must be sure we are personally born again—that our basis of confidence for attaining eternal life is Jesus Christ and Him alone. Salvation is trusting Christ to do for us what we could never do for ourselves—forgive our sins and make us members of God's family.

The new birth is but the beginning of a spiritual life characterized by a growing relationship with God. Because we have a loving heavenly Father, we can CAST our cares upon the Lord with four types of prayer.

*C*onfession means agreeing with God about our shortcomings, being honest and open with Him. We can ask God for forgiveness just as we would a friend whom we have wronged.

The Holy Spirit is the great Changer of teachers. One of the most beautiful things we can model before our students is what the Holy Spirit is doing in our lives.

*A*doration is worshiping God for His attributes. How

many descriptive words about God can you name? He is always-existing, all-controlling, all-powerful, everywhere-present, all-knowing, all-righteous, all-truthful, all-loving, and never-changing.

Adoration of God's attributes helps us appreciate who He is and who we are in relationship to Him. For example, because God is all-knowing, we can't hide anything from Him. Nor can we surprise Him, either, by anything we think or do. We should feel secure in our relationship to One who decided to love us knowing everything about us.

Supplication means making our or others' needs known to God. Personal petition acknowledges our dependence on God for our daily needs. As teachers, we also need wisdom, openness to the Holy Spirit of creativity, and sensitivity to the spirits of our students.

It's also good to ask the Lord to build a fire of love and enthusiasm in us for each session. Whatever else happens in our Sunday schools, we must be fostering positive attitudes, even enthusiasm, for God and His Word.

Keep a personal and class prayer diary, listing requests and how God answers. Jot down dates for each, too, and be sure to thank Him. Assign different prayer concerns and students to each day of the week. Prayer helps us focus more clearly on God's goals for us and our students as revealed in His Word, the Bible. Ask God for wisdom and understanding regarding the Bible portion to be taught.

Thanksgiving expresses our gratitude for God's good gifts. We can read Bible prayers (such as Philippians 1:9-11 or Ephesians 3:14-21) aloud as our own, inserting our or a student's name. After praying, we don't sit back and expect God to do all we desire. As co-laborers with God, we have responsibilities as well. Only after Moses raised his stick over the Red Sea did God part the water. We do what we can, and let God do all we can't. We can study and prepare; God has to give us wisdom. We can talk during a lesson; God has to convict students to change attitudes and actions.

Are you excited about teaching? Do you thank God daily for the privilege He has given you of teaching the Bible? As Sunday school teachers, we are involved in one of

"I wish you'd study your lesson *before* we leave for Sunday school!"

the world's greatest enterprises, worthy of our highest priority.

Look Down into the Bible

Think of teaching the Bible as the top rung of a ladder with five lower rungs. Ranked from the easiest to the hardest, these five steps to teaching would be: *hear, read, study, memorize,* and *apply* the Bible.

We *hear* Scripture by regular attendance at church. How can we expect our students to stay for the worship service if we don't? Many teachers find that taking notes helps them get more from the message.

Reading the Bible should be a daily delight, not just a duty. It's helpful to get in the habit of taking simple notes as we read, such as making up our own title for a Bible chapter. Titles can be written in a Bible margin or listed in a notebook. Good titles don't have to be profound or clever but should be short (about four words) and capture the main idea(s) of the passage. Ephesians 1 might be titled "Redemption by the Trinity."

If a chapter is too complex, first title its paragraphs or major divisions. For example, James 1: verses 1-11, "External Trials to Test;" verses 12-18, "Internal Temptations to Sin;" verses 19-27, "Hearing and Doing God's Word." Combining these three ideas produced "Trials; Temptations; Doing Word" for a chapter title. Note that a title doesn't have to be a sentence, and small connecting words can be omitted.

Titling helps us get more from our reading and gives us a grip on God's big ideas. A quick look at our list of chapter titles reminds us, within seconds, of what that Bible book is about.

Reading gives us a skeleton for Scripture; *study* adds meat to the bones. Bible study is simply digging deeper than reading. And the best tools to use are six questions: who? what? when? where? why? and how?

Some make notes about all six questions as they read a passage. Others answer one or two questions with each reading of a Bible book, chapter, or paragraph.

- *Who* are the major characters?
- *Who* is the human author? What do we learn about him from his writing?
- *What* are the major activities or ideas? List them in order or try to summarize them in one sentence.
- *What* are some key words in the text?
- *When* is the historical setting of this passage?
- *Where* are the major places? Take a moment to locate them on a Bible map or read about them in a Bible dictionary.
- *Why* is this in the Bible? What would we be missing if we didn't have this passage?
- *How* can we use it? It's deadening to our spiritual welfare just to accumulate a lot of Bible facts without accompanying personal application. It's important to jot down something specific we plan to do as a result of our Bible reading or study.

It's also good to write down questions we have. These might be factual questions regarding people we can't readily identify, dates and customs we would like to know more about, or strange words to be defined. Or we might have implicational questions.

If our questions are recorded now, we can answer them in more detailed study later. How do we proceed to find some answers when we are are ready to track them down?

Cross-references in a study Bible will help; so will a good Bible dictionary or Bible encyclopedia. Tough questions might require a commentary on the passage we are studying. Don't overlook the value of a standard encyclopedia set for answering some Bible questions.

On the next page is a sample form to copy and use to record Bible study notes. Not every chapter or paragraph gives all this information. Sometimes no people are mentioned; other times no places, and so on. We don't have to use the whole form; nor do we have to complete it in one or two sittings. Digging directly in the Bible gold mine first helps us better understand and appreciate the helps found in curriculum.

Mastering memory verses ourselves is the best way to motivate students to learn them. When new curriculum is received, it's helpful to put all the memory verses for the quarter on cards to carry in our pocket or purse. If we look at the verses in spare moments and concentrate on them just before going to sleep, we'll be amazed at how well we know them in class.

Don't forget that the Holy Spirit is the One who makes the Bible come alive for us as well as for our class. Start a study session by praying, "Open my eyes, that I may behold wonderful things from Thy law" (Psalm 119:18, NASB*). Thank God for what you have learned from His Word, and ask His help to apply it.

For a more detailed treatment of hearing, reading, studying, memorizing, and applying Scripture, see the author's *Getting More from Your Bible* (Victor Books).

New American Standard Bible.

Major characters: _____

_____

_____

○ _____

Author: _____

_____

Major activities: _____

_____

_____

Key words: _____

_____

_____

Historical setting: _____

_____

○ _____

Major places: _____

_____

_____

Why this is in the Bible: _____

_____

_____

How can I use this?: _____

_____

_____

What I plan to do: _____

_____

○ _____

My questions: _____

_____

_____

Personal Bible study notes

Applying the Bible personally before teaching it to others leads us to the third look.

Look In to Our Hearts

Teachers are to be like trees, not pipes. We should not just convey the Bible but be changed by it. As we absorb its spiritual sustenance, we blossom with fruit that blesses others. It's better to be a living letter than just a blaring loudspeaker.

We should ask questions not only of the Bible, but also of ourselves. SPECS forms an acrostic reminder of five questions to analyze our attitudes and actions in the light of God's Word. Does this passage show me any:

- Sins to forsake?
- Promises to claim?
- Examples to follow?
- Commands to obey?
- Stumbling blocks to avoid?

It's also good to ask, "What should I do now?" and choose at least one thing we can do today to grow in Christlikeness.

Look Out at Our Students

Do we view students as problems or potentials? Jesus selected His first twelve disciples as raw material, knowing what He could do with them as the Master Teacher over the next three years. Jesus' clear-cut *aims* for His students determined His *activities* with them.

What do you want to accomplish this Sunday in your class? It has been well said, "Aim at nothing, and you're likely to hit it." Often verbal buckshot is blasted at students, with the hope that some of the pellets will strike nerves of need.

Select aims for every session to be led. An aim is simply a clear statement of what we want to accomplish.

We need aims to:

- Know what to include (and exclude) in our lessons
- Guide our choice of teaching methods
- Use our class time most wisely
- Evaluate how well we have done at teaching

Good aims are *specific, measurable,* and *attainable.* That our students be better Christians is an admirable goal, but how will we know if and when that happens unless we define what specific aspects of being a better Christian we want them to adopt?

"That each student will read his Bible" sounds specific, but how much? How often? Starting when? Success is measurable if we specify a chapter a day for the next seven days.

Reading three chapters daily for the next 365 days is specific and measurable but probably not attainable. One chapter a day for seven days is practical enough to be attainable (and begin what we hope will become a daily habit).

Aims are either *mental* (what do I want my students to *know?*), *emotional* (what do I want my students to *feel?*), or *volitional* (what do I want my students to *do?*). These types of aims pertain to students' accumulation of information, attitudes about that information, and actions springing from personal choices, respectively.

In lesson planning, selecting only those items that lead to stated aims requires the art of omission. Liken each lesson to a rocket blasting toward a target, eliminating any excess baggage that will slow it down. Block any detours that might deter it from its destination. Bible writers' aims guided their selection (and deletion) of material. Read the last two verses of John chapter 20, for example.

One benefit of curriculum is its total correlation with stated goals. Most teachers' manuals suggest both unit and lesson aims with lesson material carefully chosen to help reach them.

Every part of a lesson plan should be correlated to contribute to the central aim(s), whether Bible study, worship time, enrichment ideas, songs, Scripture readings, student manuals, or take-home papers.

The Bottom Line

In later years, what will our students remember most about us? Though the Holy Spirit can recall lesson content for them when necessary, they will tend to remember our attitudes. What overall impression are our students building by weekly exposure to us? May their later thoughts be:

- "I wish I could know the Lord as well as he does."
- "He liked me; he was my friend."
- "She believed in me."
- "She was excited about Jesus."

Teaching is more than a mental exercise of preparing and presenting a lesson. It takes continual personal development as we look *up* to the Lord, *down* to the Bible, *in* to our hearts, and *out* to our students.

Looking in each direction before you teach will help you to be the best Sunday school teacher you can be.

2

Motivation: Loving Students

We teach some by what we say.
We teach more by what we do.
We teach most by what we are.

Much in Christianity is caught more than it is formally taught. The Master Teacher shows us by His example that being the best Sunday school teacher involves loving our students and building strong relationships with them.

Jesus chose the Twelve so that they might be with Him and that He might send them forth to teach (Mark 3:14). He built quality into a few as they shared life for about three years. Of course, Jesus embodied perfect Christianity as the God-man. We need to let our pupils get to know us outside the classroom as real people who love the Lord, struggle with problems, and have some victories and even some defeats.

We want our students to love Jesus most of all, but we are His representatives and models. A good shepherd knows his sheep, and they know him. Successfully ministering teachers know and care about each student, teaching individuals, not just classes. We are to communicate with people, not just cover the curriculum.

Strong personal relationships between teacher and students intensify the teaching-learning process. Pupils listen more closely to someone they love and desire to please. They later recall most readily teachers who showed a personal interest in them.

During the next three minutes, see how many adjectives you can jot down about your class as a group. . .

Well—how did you do? Did the thoughts flow fast, or did you have to struggle?

Something to think about: What adjectives would our pupils jot down about us if each were asked? Would their list include words meaning *warm, friendly, caring,* and *helpful?*

How can we get better acquainted with our students and motivate them?

We Can't Say It Enough Ways

Be a friend to students. Express appreciation to class members orally, in writing, and through actions.

Notice and comment on how well they are acting or what they are wearing. Praise attitudes and character traits we want to reinforce. Flattery is false; true appreciation is honest and sincere. Ignore what we want to disappear; don't reward bad behavior by public recognition. Nor should we ever criticize a student in the presence of his peers.

Remember birthdays and other special events in their lives. A homemade card signed by each class member helps build good relationships among them. Let absentees know they are missed, without prying for reasons. Sometimes call just to see how their week is going.

Occasionally give small rewards for good behavior or jobs well done. Don't be afraid of an occasional hug or physical pat on the back if it's spontaneous and natural.

Structure class time so it's not just a group experience. Plan to meet alone with each student by having teaching assistants help individuals memorize Bible verses. Or prearrange for teen or adult class members to come to younger departments for ten minutes to meet each student.

Use examples from daily life, changing stories to involve hobbies and interests of members. Give specific examples of how truth would apply to their age level without identifying individuals. Ask them to share illustrations. Have they ever known people who are cruel to others, for example?

Schedule around their priorities, and attend some of

their activities (sports, school plays, or talent shows). Engaging in fun activities with pupils tells them we are interested in them as people, accepting them as they are without ulterior motives.

We're Ready When You Are

Be available for informal interchange with early arrivers. We can't scurry around making last-minute preparations and concentrate on our students.

The best teachers head off many discipline problems by preliminary conversation and by recruiting helpers. List some of the ways active members could help before, during, and after class. I can vividly recall how thrilled I was to be a "teacher's assistant" for Mr. Frazier (seventh grade) and Miss Kohout (ninth grade).

Encourage others to talk about themselves by asking questions, and show interest in them by being a good listener. Have some key questions in mind to ask others to deepen the relationship, remembering always to use general questions with strangers or casual acquaintances. An open-ended question ("Can you tell me about your family?") allows an answer at whatever level is desired.

The Dale Carnegie Course in Public Speaking, Human Relations, and Leadership Skills (highly recommended; source addresses are on page 133) asks participants to conjure up a mental image of a *house* with a chimney. Then imagine a *work glove* waving from the chimney. The glove is holding a *tennis racket*, which is swatting a *dog*. In the dog's mouth is the handle of a *suitcase* containing *blueprints*. Can you guess what life areas these mental images symbolize?

Give proper facial responses (nod, smile, frown) or appropriate grunts and "uh huhs." Sharing ourselves means avoiding a one-way interrogation. Reflecting back a little on what the other said draws out more about the subject. "Oh, he fixed your bike?"

If we meet a pupil when we're hurried, say we can give two or three minutes of undivided attention, and do so.

Keep confidences. Leaking private information is one

Topics for conversational questions

of the fastest ways to destroy a relationship and discourage anyone from opening himself to us.

Listen to their interactions with each other. Knowing we have pupils wild about horses or racing games helps us prepare lessons and illustrations that more effectively communicate with them.

Unhurried prayer time with a class can surface many needs and concerns. Occasionally use a bag containing slips of paper labeled with topics for prayer or praise (family, God, toys, pets, friends, school). In conversational prayer, each member gives praise or makes a petition for the topic drawn from the bag.

Intercessory prayer for each pupil reminds us of his needs and makes him more precious to us. It's easy to remember the name and be concerned about someone for whom we pray regularly.

We Did It

One of the best ways to get to know students is to engage in meaningful projects together both in and out of class. The best projects relate to current lessons and involve every member.

One Sunday school class made a videotape of David's encounter with Goliath. Planning ahead, they made props and costumes and enlisted outsiders and parents to help them with the actual shooting. Another creative teacher and her students designed a slide presentation to tell Joseph's story. They had fun working on the script and posing for the slides. "But that takes a lot of time," someone objects. What worthwhile accomplishment in life doesn't require lots of commitment?

Class activities need not be on such a grand scale. Try something as simple as making a newspaper from the time of current lessons. Recast the Scriptures as news stories, cartoons, want ads—any item one might find in a newspaper. Collecting and photocopying them is an incidental extra to the happy group learning experience.

Many other tried-and-proved Bible learning activity suggestions are given in chapters 3 through 10.

Notice each person's work, commenting positively on it. Display their work in the classroom, and show it off to others. Be excited about their developing skills and knowledge. When I stopped being most excited about what I was doing, I was free to focus on my students. The more I get them involved in teaching and learning, the greater their (and my) joy.

That's a Good Question

Children have an innate curiosity given by their Creator. We want to encourage their investigation about God and His Word and discourage it about evil. Ask for their comments, and wait for their answers. Draw out their opinions. "What do the rest of you think about this?"

Ask good questions that require more than a one-word answer, and listen attentively as students respond. The more at home we are in our material the more we can concentrate on others, instead of thinking about what we are going to say in the next lull. If no one has an answer, ask increasingly simpler questions until someone answers.

Ask the Holy Spirit to guide the students as well as the teacher during class time. In a class climate of warm acceptance, questions and comments don't always come at ideal times. Sometimes a short answer will suffice for now. God can give instant insight as to how much time to allot to the unexpected.

Repeat softly-spoken questions or comments when necessary. We never want to make anyone feel foolish for asking any question. Even if classmates laugh at one of their peers, we must be careful to encourage the questioner's spirit.

Questions tell us a lot about what our students are thinking. Of course the more time we spend with them, the more comfortable they will feel with us.

Give credit for any answer given or the thought that produced it. To incorrect answers (if not an opinion question), we might respond, "That's a good point, but I'm looking for something else," or, "That's one of the best non-right answers."

A good teacher is a good listener, treating students with respect. Some teachers recruit a class secretary to record class questions and comments for them.

It's in the Book

Make a notebook page about each student, including a photo (taken yourself, if necessary).

How much of the following information do you know about each student? ☐ Nickname ☐ Address and phone number ☐ Birthday ☐ Special abilities and interests ☐ School ☐ Parents' names and occupation(s) ☐ Other family members ☐ Home conditions ☐ Hobbies ☐ Physical characteristics ☐ Favorite books, sports, heroes ☐ Other church involvements ☐ Commitment to Christ and spiritual growth ☐ Attitudes expressed ☐ Reasons for attending Sunday school.

After conversations and home visits, record insights in

Photo of student

Name _____
Nickname _____
Address _____
Phone _____
Birthday _____
School _____

- Abilities and interests _____
  _____
- Parents _____
  _____
- Other family members _____
- Home conditions _____
  _____
- Hobbies _____
  _____
- Physical characteristics _____
  _____
- Favorite books, sports, heroes _____
  _____
- Church involvements _____
  _____
- Commitment to Christ _____
  _____
- Attitudes expressed _____
  _____
- Reasons for attending _____
  _____
- My goals _____
  _____
- Prayer requests _____

the notebook. Also include goals for the student and prayer requests.

Hey, You in the Orange Shirt!

What joy is evident on students' faces when they are greeted by name.

The three keys of *impression, repetition,* and *exaggeration* can help us and our class members remember names. A new name needs a strong first impression, but it often comes across like a ball of fuzz. Ask the person to repeat it slowly, then try pronouncing it. Get the correct spelling. I once received a letter addressed to Tari Hawl after I'd misspelled the sender's name in correspondence.

Learn each person's name and what it means (consult an unabridged dictionary). Visualizing a spiritual goal based on the name's meaning gives the person something to live up to. *Karen* means "pure one," for example.

Repeat individual names in discussion and prayer. Put names and a short personal note on papers to be given out.

Take composite or individual pictures of a large class, and make a name key on a separate sheet to study between sessions. It would be ideal for each member to have a copy.

If class name tags are used, print them boldly and large enough to be read from the front of the room. It's difficult to maintain discipline if we have to call members by shirt or blouse colors.

Anyone's name, biblical or modern, can form an exaggerated pictured as a memory crutch. For Artaxerxes, imagine a man having a *heart attack* because he's *exerting* himself too much ("Heart-tack-xerxes"). Some names are easier than others. For my name, picture a large *terry* towel coming down a narrow *hall* (Terry Hall). Abercrombie is *a bird* giving a *crumb* to a *bee.*

How might your name be pictured? And those in your class? For fun, give a teen or adult class two minutes to exaggerate each other's name by pairs.

Involving a physical feature of the person in his or her name can backfire. Pastor Kelly had a big stomach, but imagine the embarrassment of the person who greeted him as Pastor Belly.

What if we can't recall a name when we meet the person again? We should swallow our pride and ask because they've probably forgotten ours, too.

The United Way

Wise Sunday school teachers who yearn to accelerate the effectiveness of their teaching of God's Word will seek parental cooperation. We should view our task as not only to train children but also to help train parents in how to guide their children toward God and good.

Send periodic thank-you notes to parents for getting their children to church on time, encouraging review of memory verses, and so on. Highly valued by many parents is a monthly or quarterly letter from their child's teacher explaining content to be covered (with dates), lesson aims, memory passages, possible ways the truth might relate to everyday life, and some creative review suggestions. Some of this could be taken from the curriculum. Suggest take-home papers be placed in a binder and reviewed with another family member.

The same letter could be duplicated for all, with a personal note of each child's achievements. Be positive; don't document in writing any suggestions for improvement.

Also provide parents with a calendar of class, departmental, or church activities at least one month ahead (three is better) for family planning.

Home visits are vital to get to know and understand a student and his parents. Aim to visit at least twice a year. For the initial contact, take Eva Cornelius's excellent suggestion to make an appointment for thirty minutes to share the goals of your Sunday school for their child. Impress on the parents that we are only their assistants.

Let them know how glad we are to have their son or daughter in class. Say we want to do two things with the child: (1) lead him to confess Christ as Savior and Lord, and (2) lay a foundation to help him live a truly Christian life.

Be sensitive to the parents' level of spiritual interest. Ask if they would like to do goal 1 or have you do so when the child is ready. Offer to teach them how to do it.

Stress the importance of prompt and regular attendance. When away, they can visit another Sunday school and send a note for credit. Show how to best review the lesson from take-home papers by role playing with the student. Encourage them to notice and compliment any handwork and ask questions to help in review.

Encourage commitment to daily Bible reading and devotions suited to the family members' age levels and interests. Provide or guide their selection of helpful resources (such as *Finally, Family Devotions That Work,* from Moody Press).

Invite parents to visit class at least once. Perhaps they will help with discipline and memorization.

A friendly telephone contact with parents is good, too. In a class of ten, one call a week puts you in touch with each home five times a year. Chat positively about the pupil's progress. Mention any special events. Inquire about evidences of Christian growth he is showing at home. Thank parents for the privilege of working with them in the Christian education of their children.

Also meet quarterly with others who are working with the same age group in other church ministries.

It Only Takes One

Most people already feel inferior and needn't be reminded of it. One of the main reasons I'm in the ministry today is because during the ninth grade, at a time when I was quite discouraged, one person greatly influenced me. I had failed miserably at a public part in a youth group program at church. After getting through my speech, I dropped all my note cards on the platform. Everyone laughed, while I died inside.

Later that evening an older minister put his arm on my shoulder and asked if I'd ever thought about being in the ministry. I was shocked. Definitely not, especially after my poor performance in public, scattering cards before 200 laughing people. Others were too embarrassed to talk with me, but he encouraged me, praised what I had done right, and told me how I could tape my cards into my Bible.

Love is the greatest glue for relationships. After all, isn't that how God mainly builds a relationship with us and motivates us? What's our response when we realize how much God loves us? A student will do almost anything for a teacher who truly loves him.

A century ago John Milton Gregory summarized successful teaching in seven classic statements called *The Seven Laws of Teaching* (reprinted in 1954 by Baker Book House). The first is: "The teacher must know that which he would teach and those whom he would teach."

Knowing your students as well as your subject will help you to be the best Sunday school teacher you can be.

3

Anticipation: Using Curiosity

What teacher wouldn't like students to arrive early for class, eager to learn? If such is not our situation, guess who's fault it probably is. Point one finger at a problem, then look closely at the remaining three aimed at the usual cause. Fortunately, the extended thumb points up to the Problem Solver.

Jesus was a master at building curiosity for what He wanted to teach. Recall how He confounded the Jewish lawyers in the Temple at age twelve (Luke 2:46-47) and how He prodded Nicodemus's curiosity by the cryptic statement, "You must be born again" (John 3:7). Jesus piqued the interest of the woman at the well by claiming to have water that could quench one's thirst forever (John 4:13-14).

Teachers can't assume students are motivated just because they are in Sunday school or attending a Bible class. It's the teacher's task to raise the students' expectation level. Let's give them a good reason to come back—other than that it's Sunday again—by building anticipation and exciting curiosity in students for a learning experience. Below are some ways to accomplish this; there are many others.

Hide Some Pieces

Cover a picture of any familiar scene (Bible or modern) with a piece of heavy paper that has some puzzle-shaped "windows" cut in it. Students will guess what the whole picture might be as the windows are opened one by one and clues are revealed. When preparing, hold the cover paper over the picture against a window or lighted overhead projector, if necessary, so puzzle windows are cut over key elements of the picture beneath. Hinge the cut-outs with tape on one side so each can be opened easily.

What Bible event involving a lot of animals might be depicted in the scene above? Noah's ark is a good guess, even though it is wrong. The answer is on page 47.

The need to see the big picture of a subject can be emphasized by giving each student one connecting piece of a jigsaw puzzle and asking him to find other members whose pieces mate to his. After members guess what the whole picture might be, display the puzzle box lid.

For younger ones, use gently-curving cuts to divide a teaching picture for them to assemble during presession.

Leave the Ending Open

Stop at a crucial point in a story, leaving the group "hanging on the cliff" until the next meeting. It needn't always be a Bible story; sometimes use an illustration from personal experience. Ideally, the story should illustrate the main principle from the current or next lesson, since it will be remembered so well. This method works best, of course, if students don't know the ending.

For example, one of the most significant events of my college days involved girls:

> Before my first Christmas vacation I received a "Dear Terry" letter from my girl friend at home 400 miles away, leaving me disenchanted with girls. When I received a letter from a student nurse inviting me to be her blind date at a banquet, I wondered if I should go. After looking at her picture in the student directory, I still wasn't sure. She had super-short hair and was so thin that if she had gotten a run in her nylons, she would have fallen out! Plus, a "free" date can be very costly after factoring in suit cleaning, flowers, transportation, and after-dinner entertainment. I took a poll among my friends and decided to risk it. On May 5th, when I went to the door of her home, what a surprise when the door opened. I was at a loss for words or what to do next. I was shocked! But the conclusion of the story will have to wait until our next session.

Get extra mileage in the next lesson by starting with the unfinished story and dropping it abruptly again until later in the hour. When a story is continued over a week or more, ask questions as review. Provide correlated pictures for younger ones to color or trace.

A Strange Story with a Hidden Meaning

> Imagine that you went hunting and took with you an *old bow*. You shot at a box of *Jello*. But you missed because the Jello was moving on

the back of a *whale*. You also missed because, just as you took aim, up in front of you came *a mist* of water. The mist came from a *hose* that someone turned on you. Your arrow completely overshot to the opposite shore and landed in a mineral called *mica*. The water between you and your only arrow was all *icy*. But you dove in anyway, and you soon became *numb*. When you got to the other side there was a big pair of eyes watching your only arrow. So you crept up behind this creature and did carefully *zip an eye*, one at a time. The eyes belonged to a huge *bull-frog*. He couldn't move anyway because he *had a backache*.

The story itself is easy to learn, but there is a disguised meaning hidden in it. Can you guess the subject of this picture of the story? A class doesn't need to see a printed picture. It works as well, if not better, for each person to just use his imagination.

Strange picture with a hidden meaning

For extra fun and learning, tell the story again, pausing before each italicized word for members to recite aloud the missing piece (or whisper it to a partner). During another telling of the story with pauses, ask each person to recall the missing piece silently while you make a suitable hand or body motion as suggested below.

□ *Old bow:* pretend to hold a hunting bow in one hand and draw back its string with the other. □ *Jello:* touch two thumbs together with index fingers extended vertically to form three sides of a box. □ *Whale:* sweep both hands together across in front. □ *A mist:* lift open hands, palms up, in front of face. □ *Hose:* pretend to hold and aim a hose with both hands. □ *Mica:* extend one index finger in arch and down like arrow path. □ *Icy:* pat air in several places with palms down. □ *Numb:* clench fists, grit teeth, and quiver. □ *Zip an eye:* pretend to pull a zipper across one eye. □ *Bullfrog:* put hands on hips and puff out cheeks. □ *Had a backache:* put hands on lower back as though aching.

Do you know the deeper significance of this story? Perhaps you think it's a list of the minor prophets. That's an excellent guess, but it's something else. Here is the answer key:

The story helps us learn the pre-Exile prophetic books of the Old Testament in chronological order. There are eleven Bible books tucked into the story. Pronunciation of transitional links are given in italics. □ Old bow: *ole bow diah*, Obadiah □ Jello: *jell ole*, Joel □ Whale: symbolic of Jonah □ A mist: *a miss*, Amos □ Hose, *hose ay ah*, Hosea □ Mica, Micah □ Icy, *ice say ah*, Isaiah □ Numb, *nay umb*, Nahum □ Zip an eye, *zip an eye ah*, Zephaniah □ Bullfrog: Jeremiah (ever hear the song "Jeremiah was a bullfrog"?) □ Had a backache, *ha back uk*, Habakkuk.

I struggled with remembering and teaching this information until one student invented the story and another drew the picture. Teachers needn't come up with all of the creativity themselves. Get students excited about creative thinking, and commit them to the Holy Spirit of creativity. You will be amazed and overjoyed at what they will do.

Can You Guess These Two?

Here is a riddle to solve. Jeremy was packing his suitcase for a vacation trip and wanted to take along the following items: a book, some cleanser, a companion, a large quantity of gold, a hammer, some honey, a lamp, medicine, milk, meat, a mirror, some seeds, a song, a sword, and lots of water. The problem is he only had room for one of those things. But Jeremy figured out how to pack *all* of the above items in his bag by putting in *one* thing. What is the thing he packed?

(The answer is a Bible.)

Here is a more difficult riddle by an anonymous author.

> God made Adam out of dust,
> But thought it best to make me first;
> So I was made before the man,
> According to God's most holy plan.
> My whole body God made complete,
> Without arms or hands or feet.
> My ways and acts did God control,
> But in my body He placed no soul.
> A living being I became,
> And Adam gave to me a name.
> Then from his presence I withdrew,
> For this man Adam I never knew.
> All my Maker's laws I do obey,
> And from these laws I never stray.
> Thousands of me go in fear,
> But seldom on the earth appear.
> Later, for a purpose God did see,
> He placed a living soul in me.
> But that soul of mine God had to claim,

And from me He took it back again.
And when this soul from me had fled,
 I was the same as when first made;
Without arms, legs, feet, or soul,
 I travel on from pole to pole.
My labors are from day to night,
 And to men I once furnished light.
Thousands of people both young and old,
 Did by death bright lights behold.
No right or wrong can I conceive;
 The Bible and its teachings I can't believe.
The fear of death doesn't trouble me;
 Pure happiness I will never see.
And up in heaven I can never go,
 Nor in the grave or hell below.
So get your Bible and read with care;
 You'll find my name recorded there.

(The answer is a great fish, such as the one that swallowed Jonah.)

Curious Questions

Teaser questions can build curiosity about coming subjects. Suppose this is the last Sunday of the current quarter, and next week we begin a study of the book of Proverbs. My presentation might include the following:

> You have in your possession a book with more practical insight into life's questions than you realize. In that book, God says there are twelve things He specifically hates. Do you know what they are?
>
> What one thing can a wife do which will almost guarantee she will make her husband successful?
>
> There are several kinds of fools. One type should be helped; another is beyond hope and should be avoided. Do you know the difference between the two? How could we teach our children to recognize those who can be helped and those who can't?

How would you recognize a "strange woman" or woman of the street?

How could we teach a child to recognize a wicked or slothful man?

How can we help assure that our child will make the right choices when apart from us?

There is a way most church feuds could be eliminated if just one thing was done. What is it?

How can we avoid ever being kidnapped?

Why should we place curbs on our curiosity and that of our children?

Some parents should definitely not help their children get education beyond high school. How do you know if your child is in that category or not?

How can a fool parade as a wise man and get away with it?

What sin is committed by many Christians, putting them in the same category as a rebel or a saboteur?

Why should we not loan money to poor people?

What is often done in churches which is like trying to chew on a sore tooth or run on a broken foot?

How can you tell what kind of person your son or daughter wants to be deep in his or her heart?

Did you know that all of the answers to these questions and many more like them are found in the book of Proverbs? Here is a handout list of these questions. Use it as you read Proverbs. Next quarter's classes will discuss the answers from God's Book of Wisdom, Proverbs.

It's often best to read the questions, then give the class a list of them on a handout.

Once older classes catch the concept, they will enjoy making up such questions as a Bible reading technique.

Clues and Other Questions

Can you guess this Bible character?

- Existed before the earth was created (Job 38:4-7)
- Spirit being who lives forever (Hebrews 1:13-14; Luke 20:36)
- Helped answer Daniel's prayer (Daniel 8:16)
- God's first spokesman in the New Testament (Luke 1:19)
- Predicted two miraculous births (Luke 1:13, 19, 26-31)
- Left a man speechless in the temple (Luke 1:18-20)
- Name means "Hero of God"
- Told Mary she would be the virgin mother of Jesus (Luke 1:26-35)
- One of God's angelic messengers (Luke 1:19, 26)
- Name begins with letter G

Note how the clues get increasingly easier. (The answer is Gabriel.)

Thought questions may be factual. Why are 2, 10, 20, and 613 all correct answers for how many commandments God gave at Mount Sinai? (Jesus summarized them all in 2 great commands; God wrote the first 10 on stones; Moses broke the tablets and received them again; there were a total of 613 commands issued at Sinai [Exodus 20; Numbers 10:9].)

Why did God pick 70 as the number of years for Judah's Babylonian captivity? (By the number of sabbatical years His people had robbed during the 820 years they lived in the Promised Land [2 Chronicles 36:20-21])

Why was the number 40 chosen for the years the Hebrews would wander in the wilderness? (One year for each day the spies had spent checking out the land of Canaan in unbelief [Numbers 14:32-35])

Assign interesting things to look for as students read a passage, such as in Genesis 1-5:

- Man with the first permanent identification mark
- World's first polygamist

- Oldest man in the world
- 365-year-old man who disappeared while taking a walk with God
- Founder of Nineveh (where Jonah later preached)
- Couple who had their first child after being married 500 years

(Answers are Cain, Lamech, Methuselah, Enoch, Nimrod, and Noah and his wife, respectively.)

Or consider these humorous questions from the first five chapters of the Bible:

- Which came first, the chicken or the egg?
- What time of day did God create Adam?
- How do we know computers were used in the Garden of Eden?
- What did Adam and Eve do after they left Eden?

Generate curiosity with grocery bags.

(Answers are the chicken; a little before eve (Eve); Eve said to Adam, "You need an Apple II" [apple, too]; they raised cain (Cain).)

It's in the Bag

Stand three large grocery bags in a prominent place in the classroom. Make the bags appear full with their tops folded closed (hold with clothespins if necessary). At each session have a mixture of humorous and serious prizes to award from the bags for volunteers and achievers. Tell the students not to think about the bags. Casually mention that they're placed in the front where they won't be distracting. Joke about what might be in the bags as class gifts. Suggest students respond to any mention of the bags by asking aloud, "What bags?"

Examples of bag items I enjoy using are:

- "Something only God has ever seen" (a peanut inside its shell)
- "Only one of its kind in the world, yet something from which we all have partaken" ("original" apple from the Garden of Eden—an apple with one large and one small bite taken. Ask class to guess which was Adam's and Eve's.)
- A book
- A gift certificate from a pizzeria or fast food restaurant
- "A prize worth about $800." ("Red Sea water" [sea water made red with food coloring]; it would cost about $800 to travel to the Red Sea to fill a jug with water.)

After the laughs (or disappointments), give the winner(s) of the humorous items a more serious prize.

You Can Do It

It's motivational to demonstrate a skill students would like to have. For example, to whet a class's appetite to make chapter titles and acrostics, first make and master the method on a Bible book or portion. Then ask the group to quiz you. Specify the Bible portion, and have them either (1) call out a chapter number for you to name its big idea or major event; or (2) call out a person doing something for you to tell what chapter. They will be impressed! Don't mind if you miss some; that will make the point that chapter titling is for the big ideas of a book.

Then say, "The exciting part that is you are all capable of doing what I just did! At the end of our next session you will be 'walking Romans' (or whatever Bible portion will be used)."

Emphasize the life benefits to be gained. "If you are here the next twelve Sundays, you'll have twelve workable methods to grow faster spiritually." Or, "You'll have six ways to win others to your way of thinking."

I have dropped this statement randomly into young adult classes. "There are six things a fellow can do for his fiancée or wife to keep her happy, head-over-heels in love with him, and glad to do 'most anything he wants for life." They will beg for the information, but I say, "There isn't time on Sundays. It takes about three hours, and I only want to present the six things as a package." After several requests, I respond, "If you're interested, let's meet at 5:00 AM on [a certain day]." I've never lacked for a sizeable crowd at those early-morning sessions. Attendance has been as high as 150! We can't build enough curiosity for our subject.

Al Did It

Can you think of a teacher (elementary, secondary school, college, or church) who highly motivated you to learn? Jot down what he or she did that we might emulate.

In tenth grade my favorite subject was plane geometry, not because I was so good at it or had a great desire for it, but because Al Lubowicki taught it. He assumed from the first day that no one liked plane geometry. His calling was to turn people who disliked plane geometry into raving fanatics about it. Mr. Lubowicki had a contagious enthusiasm about his subject and what we could do with it. Even if a homework answer was wrong, he made us feel like geniuses for getting any part of the process correct.

Challenges were among his favorite tricks. He often divided assignments into present and advanced categories, sometimes apologizing for giving us such toughies. I can remember staying up all night with two friends so we could crack the extra-credit college-level problem. As we wrote the answer in sections on the board, I can hear some of his praise for our procedure (though the answer was wrong). He made us feel so good for trying that we determined we'd get the next one correct.

One of the greatest tasks of a teacher is to be a creative motivator toward God and spiritual things.

Asking God to use you to create a fire of desire in students will help you to be the best Sunday school teacher you can be.

4

Presentation: Giving an Overview

To many Sunday school scholars (and their parents and teachers, too), the Bible is like a gigantic jigsaw puzzle. They never see the whole picture, just lots of pieces of the Bible story. Imagine the challenge, not to mention the frustration, if you could not see what the pieces formed until they were all put together.

Did you guess the whole picture from which the puzzle pieces on page 34 were taken? It's Adam naming the animals in Eden.

People pick up small parts of Bible stories from Sunday school, sermons, Bible clubs, and Bible storybooks. But not seeing how the pieces fit together makes the Bible seem overwhelming to them. Once they've seen the panoramic picture, the individual pieces make more sense.

This chapter gives two methods to teach the big picture of the Bible and its books, the first primarily for children, the latter for youth and adults. In the process, we'll demonstrate some techniques to get students actively involved in the learning process.

Ask students the questions given throughout the copy below, and write key italicized words on a chalkboard or other visual media. Visuals used should be converted to overhead transparencies for group use. For a fuller treatment of this chapter's topic, see the author's *Bible Panorama* (Victor Books).

How the Book Is Built

Here are some easy ways to remember how the Bible is put together. How many words are in the *Bible*? (2) Two words remind us of the Bible's two big parts: *Old* Testament and *New* Testament. *Testament* means a will. The Bible reveals God's will for us in an older part and a newer part.

How many letters are in the word *old*? (3) How many letters in *testament* (9). Put these two numbers side by side to remember there are 39 books in the Old Testament.

There are 3 letters in *new* and 9 in *testament*. Multiply these two numbers to get 27 books of the New Testament.

(An additional memory link for the books of the New Testament is in Christ's choice of 12 apostles. They can be divided into two groups—one of 3 [Peter, James, and John] and one of 9 [the others]. Jesus chose these men so He could multiply His ministry through them.)

Subtracting the 3 from the 9 for each testament leaves two 6s to remind us of the 66 books in the whole Bible. (Writing the above words and numbers on a chalkboard makes them even easier to grasp.)

The Bible in Three Words

The word *hep*, sometimes used by drill sergeants to keep their marching troops in step, gives us an acrostic reminder of the three topics included in the Bible:

History (past)
Experience (present)
Prophecy (future)

The history part of the Bible begins each testament. History is really "His story," the story of how God has worked in His world with the people He created. The experience books in the middle of each testament deal with how God wants to work in our lives now. Both testaments end with prophecy, a record of things God will do in the future. The Bible, then, is about what God has done, is doing, and will do.

These three topics summarize both testaments. Dividing the Bible's 66 books by 3 gives 22. There are 22 history books in the Bible (the first 17 books in the Old Testament and the first 5 in the New). To read the big story of the Bible, we need to read only one-third of its books. Note that in both testaments there are 22 supplements to the story line. (The supplements are the combined total of experience and prophecy books.)

In the Old Testament, God has emphasized the past and the future; in the New Testament, our present experience with Him and His Word is emphasized.

Old Testament Books	Topics	New Testament Books
17	History	5
5	Experience	21
17	Prophecy	1

A Bible Map for Non-Artists

The Bible story can be summarized on one easy-to-draw map. (If you or your students can draw a crooked line, you can do it.) The box on the map below shows where in the world most of the Bible's events took place.

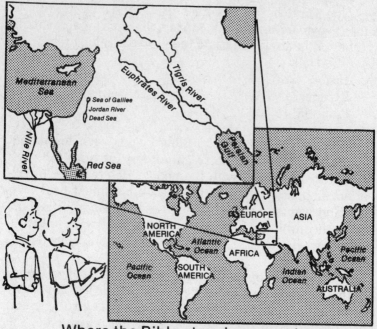

Where the Bible story happened

A silly statement helps us remember the names of the rivers and seas that bound the area: "*E.T. purrs in the red tile med.*"

Going clockwise from the upper right of the Bible map, note the Euphrates and Tigris Rivers, Persian (Purrsian) Gulf, Red Sea, Nile (rhymes with *tile*) River, and the Mediterranean Sea. The order of the E.T. rivers is easy because the top one starts with T and is closer to India, where *tigers* live. Some people who lived near the *Euphrates* were told, "*You a'fraidy of the tigers.*"

Just to the east of the Mediterranean Sea is the Sea of Galilee. The Jordan River flows out of it to the Dead Sea.

A simple short story helps us teach and draw this map.

Imagine you are looking at the bow of a fishing boat (draw lines 1, 2, and 3). The fishing lines hanging from the boat got tangled up (draw

How to draw a Bible map

lines down to 4). A boy fell out of the boat and is standing on the bottom of the shallow lake. All we see of him are his two skinny fingers under the bow of the boat (draw lines to 5). Being prepared for an emergency, he sent a balloon toward the surface, with its string trailing (draw 6 and 7). So that it doesn't ascend too fast, he hung his mitten on the string (draw 8). Ahead of the boat is the head of a water bug (draw 9). So that he can avoid all the action on his left, the bug reaches his two feelers in that direction (draw 10 and 11).

Trace your finger or pencil over the map lines several times as you reread the story. Turn away from the map and practice drawing it in the air with your finger. (You don't need to put in the numbers.) Then practice on a piece of paper or chalkboard. Name the water bodies from memory.

Look how one boy, Henry Rafacz, drew this freehand map.

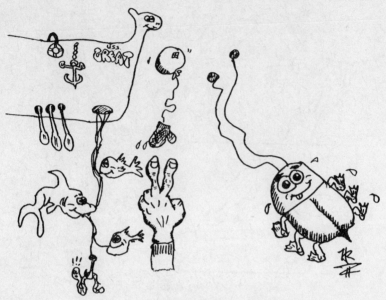

A teen's freehand Bible map

The Bible Story on One Map

Let's summarize the Bible story simply on this free-hand map. Trace over the lines and symbols on the map as they are mentioned in the story.

After God created the world, He placed Adam and Eve in the beautiful Garden of Eden (A). (Genesis says the Tigris and Euphrates rivers flowed through the Garden.) When the human family multiplied and became very wicked, God sent a great flood and later scattered people around the world from the Tower of Babel. God called Abraham and Sarah from Ur (B) to Canaan, the Promised Land (C). God made this couple the first Hebrews. (Most of the Bible was written by Hebrews; Jesus was a Jew, a later

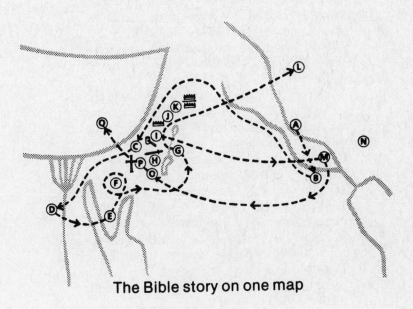

The Bible story on one map

name for the Hebrews.) The rest of Genesis records the lives of Abraham, Isaac, Jacob, and Joseph (easily remembered by their initials AI and JJ).

After the Hebrews became a great nation in Egypt (D) and were made slaves, God used ten plagues and Moses to deliver them. Their journey took them through the Red Sea to Mount Sinai (E). They were taught and tested in the wilderness (F). Then the Hebrew nation crossed the Jordan River (G) into Canaan. Three symbols summarize centuries of living there: a sword (H) for Joshua's conquest of Canaan, a gavel (I) for the many judges, and a crown (J) for the many kings. (Note Canaan has been widened to make room for the symbols.)

After King Solomon's reign, the Hebrew kingdom split in two (K), with the northern section called Israel and the southern called Judah.

After nineteen wicked kings, Israel was conquered and scattered by Assyria (L). (Its capital, Nineveh, was on the Tigris River.) Later Judah was taken into exile by Babylon (M), on the Euphrates River. Seventy years later Persia (N) conquered Babylon and allowed the Jews to return to Judah (O).

After 400 silent years, when no prophets spoke for God, Jesus came as the God-man to die on a cross for our sins (P), rise from the dead, and return to heaven.

After receiving the power of the Holy Spirit, Jesus' disciples spread the good news of a free salvation, mainly among the Jews. The apostle Paul carried the gospel to the Gentiles through many missionary journeys to the northwest of Israel (Q). He also wrote at least thirteen of the New Testament letters (part of the twenty-one experience books). The gospel is still being spread across the world by Jesus' modern disciples.

The apostle John recorded the Revelation, foretelling God's plans for the world to the end of time. The Bible ends in Revelation as it began in Genesis—with God completely in charge of His creation, with no evil opposition.

The Bible's Major Message

How well do you think you understand the major message of the Bible? What is the purpose for God's recording all this history? One good answer: To reveal God and His way of salvation.

If you had to briefly summarize the Scripture's teaching about salvation, what would you say? Any answer that gives people credit (do good, keep the Ten Commandments, obey the Golden Rule) misses the boat. The major message of the Bible is that God offers a *free gift of salvation* to all people, who are helpless to earn it on their own.

The apostle John said, "But these have been written that you may believe that Jesus is the Christ, the Son of

God; and that believing you may have life in His name" and "For God so loved the world, that He gave His only begotten Son, that whoever believes in Him should not perish, but have eternal life" (John 20:31 and 3:16, NASB).

But what does it mean to believe in Jesus? Many boys and girls familiar with Bible stories are in danger of missing eternal life and heaven by about twelve inches—the distance between the head and the heart. To know the facts about Jesus dying on a cross for our sins is not enough. We must invite Him to live in our hearts and trust Him to forgive our sins as our Savior.

I enjoy taking airplane flights. But I could stand in the airport all day telling myself how much I believe in a certain airline's planes and pilots and never get off the ground. To prove my faith in them, I have to board the plane. That's when I'm really trusting the airline to do something for me I couldn't do for myself—transport me a thousand miles in two hours.

Salvation is trusting Jesus to do something for us we could never do for ourselves—forgive our sins and give us everlasting life.

Have you ever shifted your hopes of heaven from self to the Savior? When I was in the seventh grade, I first heard the good news about Jesus' love for me. I discovered His love was so great that if I were the only sinner who ever needed a Savior, He still would have died—just for me! But His forgiveness would not be forced on me—I had to choose to receive it as a gift. Though I didn't understand it all, I acted on what little I did know. I confessed I was a sinner and began to trust Jesus to be my Savior. That was just the beginning of a whole new life—for time and eternity.

Whom or what are you trusting in?

Thank God for revealing Himself in His special Book, the Bible. Thank Jesus Christ for dying for your sins and trust Him to be your Savior. I can guarantee you from His Word—you'll be glad forever that you did.

Bible Panorama for Youth and Adults

Ask each member to choose a partner, working together by twos. Jokingly ask if each is seated near someone with whom he is on speaking terms. If not, make up, move, or meet someone new. For a humorous introduction with a larger group, ask each student to call out the name of his partner on your count of three. When the noise dies down, joke that you missed a few names, and do it again.

Ask for definitions of *trunk*. Have each pupil chose one (any) definition, and whisper it to a partner. Tell them you have a definition also. As you describe your *trunk*, each should whisper what they think your definition is to a partner. Recite each of the following, emphasizing the italicized words. "*The* trunk." "The *trunks*." "The *big* trunks." "The big *gray* trunks." "The big gray trunks *bounced!*" "The big gray trunks bounced *down the road!*" "The big gray trunks bounced down the road *as the fat man who was wearing them jogged by!*"

It's obvious that the whole sentence helps us understand the parts. And the same is true with the Bible and any of its books.

Hand out photocopies of Jonah from the *New International Version* (with NIV's chapter titles deleted; be sure to ask permission of the publisher). If your group has studied Jonah recently, use another four-chapter Bible book, such as Philippians or Ruth.

Ask each pair to join with another pair to form groups of four. Request a volunteer leader in each group (indicated by raised hand). If volunteers are slow, say the leader will be the person with the first name nearest to "J" for "Jonah." Now tell those leaders to point to whomever they want to be the leader! Remind everyone that it pays to volunteer, and ask the new leader to forgive the old one. The leader has Jonah 1 and should assign chapters 2, 3, and 4 to the other three in the small groups. Give them a few minutes to read their assigned chapter and write a summary title in four words or less.

Remind them each subgroup is reading the whole book of Jonah, but each person is reading only one chapter.

Have several volunteers read their titles, praising them for their work.

Ask if they got more from their reading because they were looking for something. If so, they experienced one of the benefits of making chapter titles.

Tell them each is about to preach a sixty-second sermon. When you say, "Go," the chapter 1 person in each group will have one minute to explain his chapter to the other three (since they didn't read it today). Have each assume the others have never heard of Jonah. They should be dramatic, making the story as interesting as possible. After one minute, call out, "Chapter 2," and so on. Have them stand in their small clusters for this.

Put the following list on the overhead (otherwise on a poster you can quickly turn over): onions, watermelon, soup, flour, relish, eggs, lettuce. Remove the list, and ask the group to recite the seven items. After they moan, show the list rearranged on the acrostic FLOWERS. Notice how much easier it became. Explain that an acrostic is a word or phrase written vertically so each letter can begin another word.

Make an acrostic together on Jonah. Ask, "What's the biggest thing in the book?" They'll probably say "fish," but if they say "Lord," use that. Let each letter of *fish* stand for a chapter of Jonah. Brainstorm together as a large group, restating Jonah titles to FISH (title for chapter 1 restated to begin with F, and so on). For example:

> **F**light from God's Call (chapter 1)
> **I**ntercession from Within Fish (chapter 2)
> **S**alvation of Nineveh's People (chapter 3)
> **H**umbling of Pouting Prophet (chapter 4)

Have each group of four make an original acrostic on Jonah. Give them thirty seconds to agree in each group on a four-letter word thematic of Jonah. FISH may not be reused. Have the leader call out the chosen word so you can list it on the board as "taken." Each group should have a different word. Remind them to work together as four on one acrostic, talking about how to restate their chapter titles to the new chosen letters. Circulate among them to offer encouragement and hints as needed.

For groups done early, have the leader coach the other three in reciting their acrostic. Have every group share their acrostic.

Ask if making acrostics wasn't easier because each had friends helping. Have each thank his three helpers.

Give the groups of four about ninety seconds to quiz each other on saying their acrostic unaided. Have several volunteers recite their acrostic.

Ask for all papers to be turned over for an oral quiz. (If your group is small or inhibited, this could be personally written.) On the following multiple-choice quiz, they have five answer choices: 0, 1, 2, 3, or 4. Have them recite the choices in unison. Suggest each be sure his partner is speaking aloud.

As you ask questions, each is to call out the first answer that comes to mind. Jokingly state, "Don't worry about saying the wrong thing. If you do, your partner will poke you and say, 'That was wrong!'" In rapid-fire fashion, ask a string of questions, such as: In what chapter of Jonah is Jonah preaching in Nineveh? What chapter has him asleep on a boat? Praying inside a big fish? What chapter has a worm chomping a vine? What chapter has the king of Nineveh announcing repentance in ashes? Sailors casting lots in a storm at sea? Jonah sulking outside Nineveh? The last question should be, "How many of you could have answered all those questions correctly yesterday?" (The answer is 0.) The students will be thrilled at how much they retained from Jonah.

Give the groups of four one minute to agree on what advice Jonah would give if he could come to our group today. They are limited to one sentence. Sharing will reveal an almost unanimous concept: "It's better to obey the Lord."

Ask each to privately consider what area of life God is repeatedly speaking to him about. Ask, "What could you do this week that would please God more than anything?" Point out that most Christians don't need more light on how to be better Christians; rather they need to obey the light they already have.

Why Use Partners?

Working by twos creates a friendly atmosphere in the group and helps each person learn more by active participation than by passive listening. Reciting to a partner helps people stay awake through a meaningful reinforcement break from listening, since the average adult attention span is about eight minutes. Using partners also provides personal accountability within a group. The larger the group, the less each person feels a need to actively participate. The best way to get each person verbalizing is to use partners. I have successfully used the partner principle with groups ranging from 2 to 2700.

For humor and efficiency, always designate who goes first when partners are to recite together. Use designators such as the one who got the most sleep last night, a volunteer (who then points to his partner and lets *him* do it), oldest, tallest, got up the earliest, has the longest hair, came the most miles to Sunday school, has the most pets, is wearing brightest shirt or blouse, or has birthday closest to today.

Beginning and Ending

Do you give your students puzzle pieces only or help them see the big picture? How do you begin a new quarter? Dive into lesson one, or take some time to motivate and orient pupils to the whole?

We should begin with the whole (Bible book, subject, current series), then week by week keep relating the parts to the whole. When we think we're done, we should look at the whole again.

Showing students the forest before and after the trees will help you to be the best Sunday school teacher you can be.

5

Investigation: Learning by Discovery

After three days, people tend to remember only 10 percent of what they read, 20 percent of what they heard, 30 percent of what they saw, 50 percent of what they saw and heard, and 60 percent of what they studied. The retention average after three days jumps to 70 percent of what was personally spoken and 90 percent of what was physically done.

Since what students say and do is retained the longest, the best Sunday school teachers get their students involved in Bible learning. Besides, it's more fun to be active rather than just passively listening during class. And just about anything goes better when we can do it with someone else.

This chapter presents ways for classes of various ages to enjoy active discovery in God's Word together. These creative Scripture projects can be used with students of all ages and with any curriculum, Scripture portion, or topic. These few samples are some of my personal favorites, and I guarantee they will work if we will but work them.

Ancient Modern News

Imagine your members are newspaper reporters during Bible times. They're to produce something that looks like a modern paper, but everything in it will be based on biblical accounts.

Read a Bible passage together, preferably in a version suited to your members' learning level.

Have sample copies of daily papers, and give the group a few minutes to scan through them to make a list of the normal items included (advertisements, business news, cartoons, domestics, drawings, editorials, fashion, filler items, headline and lead news story, interviews, letters to the editor, masthead, other news items, recipes, sports, travel, and want ads).

Have volunteers (individuals or pairs) select one item to produce from the chosen passage. Check off selections to avoid duplication.

If students are slow starting, have them look at the sample Bible newspaper items on the next page. Or have everyone do a short "want ad" to get their creative juices flowing.

You'll need paper, pencils, and crayons for each person. Give blank transparencies and overhead markers to those who will be doing any drawing (such as display ads or cartoons), making it easier to share with the larger group.

If not finished during this session, meet mid-week to complete and "publish" the composite paper. Photocopy machines make good printing presses.

A creative option would be to make a newspaper for a target audience, such as the young teens of the church or the junior department of the Sunday school. Distribute the papers with the prayer that God will use them to stimulate others to use some of these creative Bible study and sharing methods.

Making Melody

Memorizing Scripture is easy for young children, especially if set to simple, catchy melodies. Use a tape or record of Scripture set to music (such as "Sing a Song of Scripture," "Kids' Praise," or "Critter Country").

Create lyric hand motions for young children. Or form a rhythm band, using a spoon and pan or two sticks for percussion instruments. Beat on each syllable of a simple song.

Children of junior age and above can make up words to existing tunes, substituting one syllable per note. Sing

Weather: A brighter tomorrow.

The Wise Sun

"Sheds a light on life"

WISDOM SHOUTS IN THE STREETS

Wisdom, of 120 Proverbs Way, has been shouting in the streets for a hearing. She has accused the crowds along Main Street, the judges in their courts, and all the people in the land of being simpletons. She claims that they scoff at wisdom and fight facts.

When asked what basis she has for her statements, she said, "I have called you so often, but still you won't come. I have pleaded, but all in vain. For you have spurned my counsel and reproof." She also claims that Israel will experience "anguish and distress" because of its foolish choices.

Wisdom stated that when Israel calls to her when they are in trouble, she will laugh because they ignored her calling. She also claimed that all who listen to her will live in peace and safety.

NEWS BRIEFS

A man living at 2024 Greed Way robbed his parents yesterday. He took gold and silver jewelry and valuable tapestries. According to the judge, he is no better than a murderer.

A young mocker and rebel of 1925 29th St. was punished by the courts yesterday. It is hoped that others will learn from this public example.

• A murderer's conscience drove him to hell. Nobody stopped him. He lived at 2817 Death Row.

Poorman Returned

John Poorman, who was kidnapped from his 138 Poverty Ave. home, was returned safely to the Police station last night after the kidnappers realized he had no money to pay his ransom.

Apparently, after the kidnappers had gotten him to their secret hideout in the Jerusalem suburbs, they realized they had made a blunder, but they were not sure how to unkidnap him. They kept him for a week, and when they realized no money was coming, they dropped him off at the station.

Poorman, when asked how he felt, stated, "Being kidnapped and being held for ransom never worries the poor man."

Letters to the Editor

Dear Mr. Editor:
Wow! Thanks for putting into print many things that were on my heart! I really appreciate your views on righteousness. Keep it up!
—Shirley Wright

Dear Mr. Editor:
Totally disgusting! Your writing made it seem as if we are human and need divine guidance or something.
—Grate Lee Disturbed

Dear Mr. Editor:
As a student, I appreciated your advice about "trusting the Lord." I have lots of decisions and need all the help I can get.
—O. B. Dient

Ask Solomon

Dear Solomon:
I have a friend who is always unknowingly offending people. I think I should tell her, but I'm afraid I'll hurt her feelings. What should I do?
Scared 2823

Dear Scared: In the end, people appreciate frankness more than flattery.

Dear Solomon: I have a friend whom I visit quite often. We've always been close, but lately she has been giving me the cold shoulder. What's wrong?
Concerned 2517

Dear Concerned: Don't visit your friend too often, or you will wear out your welcome.

THE CURE-ALL MEDICINE

Rx A Merry Heart

the "old" song tune, counting the number of syllables in each line. For example, "Je-sus loves me, this I know" makes seven syllables. Create new sentences with the same number of syllables, and they'll work.

Different ones could be working together to write just two lines or one stanza. Others could do the chorus; then join. it all together.

Here's an example by a group of juniors using the tune from "Savior, Like a Shepherd Lead Us."

> One day many people came to Jesus,
> It was late; they were hungry.
> Jesus asked His twelve disciples,
> "How much bread and fish have we?"
> Jesus blessed it; Jesus broke it:
> The five loaves and two fishes.
> Fed five thousand, lots left over,
> Jesus fed five thousand men.

Teens and young adults with musical ability enjoy creating songs from Scripture, especially those suited for guitar accompaniment. Below is an original song by some students at Lincoln High School in Guadalajara, Mexico.

Once upon a time not so long ago
There lived a man named Jonah that you all should know.
The Lord said to Jonah, "Go and preach for me,
In that faraway land, the land of Ninevee."

Chorus:
'Way down yonder in the bottom of the sea,
'Way down yonder in the bottom of the sea,
'Way down yonder in the bottom of the sea
Lies a little, bitty fishy just awaitin' for me.
Chomp. Chomp. Chomp. Chomp. 'Ta chomp.

Jonah said, "Lord, why'd You pick on me?
I'm too tired and weak, can't You see?
Give me a little time; give me a little rest,
So when I preach the sermon I'll be more at my best."

Jonah caught an ocean liner going for a ride.
He thought he'd go to Tarshish from the Lord to hide.
He took along his sleeping bag; he thought he'd take a nap.
But the Lord said to Jonah, "Now I've got you in a trap."

The sailors started yellin'; it started getting warm.
Along came the great big, great big storm.
They threw out all the fishing tackle, then they threw the dice.
Finally they threw the preacher out at the Lord's advice.

Jonah did a jackknife, high up in the air.
He almost did a perfect dive, but to his despair,
A pair of jaws opened wide, and pretty soon he found,
He found that he was seated, seated down inside.

Jonah found a fuse box and turned on the light.
He looked for a television; none was in sight.
Instead he found a Living Bible and a note from God,
Saying, "I hope you like My submarine: I think it's kind of mod."

Three days later the fish swam in the bay,
The Lord said to Jonah, "You're getting out today.
In fifteen minutes you'll be upon the dock,
So you better preach a sermon, or at least a little talk."

Older students can also make up more sophisticated words to an existing hymn. Copy the original words, marking off the syllables, and put corresponding new syllables under them. A syllable can be "stretched" over more than one note, if necessary, but don't "bunch" two or more syllables under one note.

Here's how one teen, Ruth Hornbeck, recast Nehemiah chapter 8 to the tune of "Jesus Saves."

> "Ezra, bring the Law," they cried,
> "Read it through, read it through."
> Gather all as one to hear,
> The Word of God, the Word of God.
> Opened it for them to see;
> Blessed the Lord, the mighty God;
> Worshiped Him with humbleness.
> Praise the Lord, praise the Lord.
>
> People wept when it was read;
> Cried and cried, cried and cried.
> "Wipe those tears now right away;
> Sing and shout, sing and shout."
> "Go to eat and drink and sing;
> Make the booths to dwell therein.
> Read the Word now every day,
> To please the Lord, to please the Lord."

Let's Play a Game

An easy way to enjoy learning Bible concepts or verses is to add Bible questions to make any game a Bible learning activity. Before a player takes a turn, he has to answer one of the question cards.

Either bring some common table games to adapt to Scripture, or guide your class to design a new game "from scratch."

The whole class should read a Bible portion together first and discuss its meaning. Choose questions from a passage suitable to your students' age level. Older classes enjoy making their own questions. Provide blank 3x5 cards.

It's best to have at least twenty new questions each time you play.

Put Bible references on question cards instead of answers. When a player misses, he must look up the answer and read it aloud. He still loses his turn. But because that card is shuffled back into the playing pile, there's motivation to remember the answer.

Sometimes include extra statements on question cards: "Correct answer gives you three extra places," or, "Wrong answer sends one of your pieces back to home base."

Two teams could make questions to ask of each other. Perhaps have them categorize their questions like toothbrushes: hard, medium, and soft.

Note some of the sample student games on the next page. ☐ Using *Jeopardy*, let category and amount determine the difficulty of questions. ☐ Guess what product *Jonopoly* adapted, converting money to biblical terms and allocating portions of the playing board to Scripture passages. ☐ Using *Twister*, provide two dials, one to select a Bible chapter's question, the other to designate what part of the player's anatomy goes on the mat. ☐ *Proverbs Parcheesi* arranges the book of Proverbs into ten categories of questions, selectable by spinner. A correct answer allows the player's piece to be moved that many spaces. ☐ *Leviticus Parcheesi's* board is designed after the Old Testament Tabernacle. ☐ *John-0* teaches chapter titles or events in Bible order. ☐ Make new cards with Bible terms for *Password* by putting red color or Xs over black letters. The red window of the game sleeve masks the red overmarking. ☐ Assign a topic or number to each of the nine squares of *Tick-Tack-Toe* with corresponding questions to answer before placing an X or O. ☐ Make questions for each *chess* piece. ☐ As questions are asked of the whole group, *Saved* players may only cover a square if it contains the answer. ☐ *Barnabas hopscotch* can be chalked onto a paved area.

Crossing Words

Crossword puzzles aren't difficult to construct. Two groups (or pairs of groups) could make up crossword puz-

Bible games

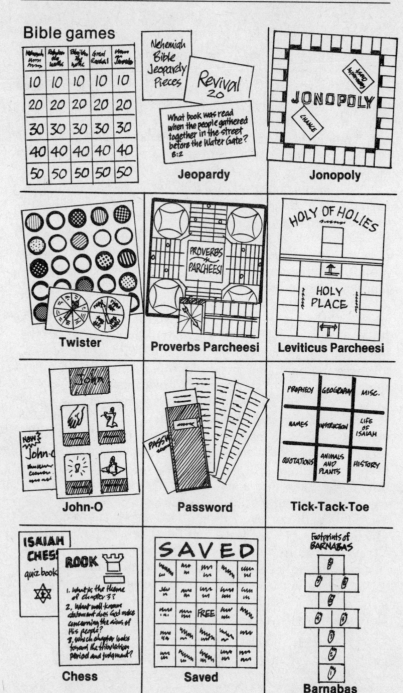

Jeopardy

Jonopoly

Twister

Proverbs Parcheesi

Leviticus Parcheesi

John-O

Password

Tick-Tack-Toe

Chess

Saved

Barnabas Hopscotch

zles for the other group to solve.

Have pupils read a passage and make a list of significant words from it (important people, places, and events). Then interlace these words Scrabble fashion on a grid sheet (sheet filled with 1/4-inch squares; hand out these). Some choose to lay a sheet of clear film (such as used for an overhead transparency) on a grid sheet, using a water-soluble marker to facilitate changes. Other classes have used the tiles from a Scrabble game to form their puzzle layout.

After getting in all possible major words, read or skim the Bible section again to see how many little filler words can be inserted. Then lay a clean grid sheet over top to trace the blank boxes for the actual crossword puzzle form. Assign numbers in order across each horizontal line at the beginning of every new word (whether it's an "across" or "down" word).

Clues can be the usual listing or a summary of the Biblical account, leaving blanks where a puzzle word occurs. For example, "God called (13 down) to preach in the city of (5 across)."

The crossword puzzle on the next page is also a Bible quiz.

The answers are on page 71.

Creative Writing About People

Have students collect information about these five categories as they read passages about a Bible person: activities, background, character, details, and example for us.

Then summarize the information creatively, such as this obituary of Barnabas by David Schnittger.

NOTED MISSIONARY DIES

A world-traveled and highly respected church leader, Joseph of Cyprus (known as Barnabas by those who knew him) died Tuesday of a short illness at an advanced age. Barnabas, a Jew of the tribe of Levi, had long been involved with a new and rapidly growing sect known as Christians. His leadership responsibilities centered mainly in the church at Antioch, but his

Bible Crossword Puzzle Quiz

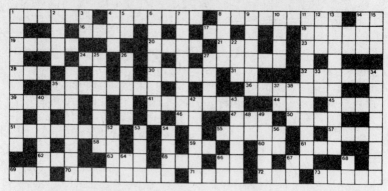

Directions: *Name the person, place, or thing called for. Then put your answer in its place in the cross-word puzzle. (Note: Thirty-one additional questions, not part of the quiz, appear near the end. Answers for these "Free Fillers" will help fill in the puzzle.)*

(Answers in King James Version)

PEOPLE
Across:
1. The third of Job's friends who came to comfort him.
41. Faithful martyr in Pergamos commended by Christ.
51. Eminent teacher in the church at Colossae.
70. Jewish name of Queen Esther.
72. Joshua's father.

Down:
1. Rebuilt the temple after the Babylonian exile.
25. Abraham married her after his first wife's death.
26. Third John was written to this man.
49. Ehud killed this fat Moabite king.
52. New Testament rendering of Abraham's first wife.

PLACES
Across:
16. One of the mountains where Israel read God's law.
23. John saw a door opened here.
30. Naaman the leper was from this country.

31. Achan's sin caused Israel's defeat at this city.
66. Where Joshua experienced his first defeat in Canaan.

Down:
4. The Jewish tribe that migrated north when it couldn't conquer its allotted portion of Canaan.
9. Country of Cyrus, who ended the Babylonian exile.
29. Where Jonah tried to flee from the Lord.
42. Greek and Roman name for Edom.
43. Asian church commanded to strengthen the things that remain.

PLANTS, ANIMALS, ETC.
Across:
19. What God sent to feed Elijah.
20. This type of person is commanded to consider the ant.
27. What David wanted to be purged with.
28. Isaiah said God would call for this from Assyria.
39. The name of a kind of serpent.
44. Moses commanded that none of this be eaten.

Down:
10. The scapegoat was to be sent out of this place.
37. Initials of two animals Jesus used in illustrations (names rhyme).
38. What God gave Abraham to replace his son on the altar.
40. Descriptive name for Satan.

PRESENTS

Across:

8. This type of person sounds a trumpet when he gives alms.

17. God promises to give us success for Bible meditation if we "observe to ____ it."

55. Second of ten plagues God gave Pharaoh.

57. What God promised King Ahaz in the virgin birth of Messiah: "The Lord himself shall give you a ____ ."

71. Jewish term for benevolent deeds.

73. What we are to perform unto the Lord.

Down:

7. Samson's kind of dedicatory vow.

11. What God has given us that is incorruptible and undefiled.

15. Number of lepers Jesus cleansed one time.

53. Kind of greeting Paul commanded believers to give one another.

POSITIONS

Across:

4. Lay ministry officers in a local church.

18. Don't appoint one of these as a church leader.

35. One chosen to take Judas' position as apostle.

36. Sihon was a king of this tribal enemy of Israel.

50. Another name for the wise men who visited the child Jesus (NASB).

62. Possessive of king of Bashan defeated by Moses.

65. We are to stand in "____" before God and sin not.

69. Spiritual relationship of Timothy to Paul.

Down:

8. The kind of living sacrifice we are to be unto God.

13. Philip had this gift and position.

FREE FILLERS

Across:

14. Initials of a Jewish kingdom and its capital city in the Old Testament.

21. First three letters of the word telling the size of the upper room.

24. First two letters of "____, live forever."

32. Another name for Moses' father-in-law.

45. Satan is the father of these.

46. Initials of two prophets ministering in Babylon during the exile.

47. Jesus was about thirty years of this when He began His public ministry.

58. Initials of two writing prophets to Israel, the northern kingdom.

59. Initials of Joseph's two sons, who became heads of Jewish tribes.

60. Interjection meaning "Look!" or "Behold!" used by Jesus.

61. What Baal's prophets did to themselves during contest with Elijah.

63. First three letters of Solomon's warning, "Be not ____ with thy mouth."

67. Initials of two of the "major" prophets in order of occurrence.

Down:

2. Rebuilt Jericho at the cost of his son as Joshua predicted.

3. Last two letters of the sister city of Sidon.

5. Name for God, usually combined with other names.

6. Church Paul addressed regarding the supremacy of Christ.

12. A Philistine giant had twelve.

14. God asked Job to explain the source of this.

22. A good reformer king of Judah.

27. What David played to soothe King Saul.

33. Initials of two of Jesus' disciples in alphabetical order.

34. Tetrarch of Abilene during John the Baptist's ministry.

35. Initials of two men who appeared from Heaven at Jesus' transfiguration.

48. Jesus' command to His disciples.

54. A Hebrew midwife (along with Shiprah) who spared Israeli newborns.

56. King of Egypt to whom Hoshea appealed for help.

64. Initials of couple killed for lying to the Holy Spirit.

66. Initials of two men who exchanged tithes and blessings after Lot was rescued.

67. Initials of two Jewish tribes sharing a common border at the Sea of Galilee.

68. Initials of a son and his father who migrated from Ur to Haran.

duties also took him to Jerusalem, Judea, and the nearby provinces of the upper Mediterranean area.

An effective teacher, prophet, church delegate, and missionary in his own right, Barnabas's chief claim to fame was in his association and travels with the acknowledged spear-head of the Christian thrust, the converted Jew Paul. Barnabas was the first church leader in Jerusalem to befriend this controversial former persecutor, and the relationship deepened through the years. As co-workers in the Antioch church, they were both recognized as natural missionary material. So they were commissioned to spread the faith to regions beyond.

After returning from their first journey, the duo was sent to represent the Antioch church at an important church council in Jerusalem, at which many landmark decisions were made.

A man of many talents, Barnabas was also a man of well-respected character. His name means "son of encouragement," and he thrived on advancing others. Though he met with some obstacles, his ministry was very effective, resulting in many new converts to Christianity and a general strengthening of the churches where he ministered.

Despite his consistent popularity, humility and deference to others were the characteristic marks of Barnabas's life.

Services for the deceased will be held at the Antioch Baptist Church, with the Reverend Apostle Paul officiating. Survivors include one sister and a nephew. Gifts and remembrances may be designated to the Judean Relief Fund.

Cheri Strahm recast Nehemiah's story into a series of letters exchanged by his enemies, titling her account, "The Sanballat Letters."

Nisan 29th
Sanballat:

Well, you were wrong. I thought we had it all sewed up, too. But some guy by the name of Nehemiah has arrived from Shushan, and he's been inspecting the walls of Jerusalem. I hear he's got the rulers and nobles on his side now. They plan to rebuild! We've got to get down there and give them some trouble. This could defeat all our plans for taking over the land.

P.S. They say this Nehemiah was cupbearer to Artaxerxes. Just what we need!

[signed] Tobiah

Elul 3rd
Comrade Sanballat:

Every prominent family in Jerusalem has been working on that wall, and you just sit back and let them! Oh, sure, we went down and mocked them, threatened them a little, and even let the Samaritan army in on the news. But what good has it done? Geshem and I think it's time for action. What kind of a leader are you? These Jews are getting out of hand.

[signed] Tobiah

Elul 10th
Sanballat:

I can't believe it. Those Jews are ready to hang the gates in the wall, and still we haven't done anything. I really think you're afraid to fight. Even with the Arabians, Ammonites, and Ashdodites on our side, you hesitated to charge the walls. Was it because of reports that Nehemiah has armed his workers? Or is it because Nehemiah prays constantly to his God? At least there are some internal problems among the Jews. Maybe that will be the answer to our problem. I hear the people are complaining about being bonded as servants. Let's see Nehemiah handle this one. He's so perfect, he makes me sick; he

won't even take his pay as governor!
    [signed] Tobiah

Elul 30th
Friend Sanballat:
    I must admit you tried. You and Geshem
tried to trick Nehemiah into leaving Jerusalem,
and you even sent him threatening letters. You
and I hired Shemaiah to prophesy against him,
and even that didn't work. So—now they've finished the wall—in only 52 days! If I weren't the
son-in-law of Shechaniah, I'd take over your job
myself. Some leader you are! The Jews are more
unified than ever since their return from Persia.
That Nehemiah, now he's a real leader type. I'm
going to begin winning over the nobles on the
inside. I think I can use my influence and get
them to turn against Nehemiah. You may not
hear from me for a while; I'm going to be busy
writing other letters.
    [signed] Tobiah

Note on the next page how some younger ones summarized what they had learned about Barnabas. One is a
scrapbook of pictures and letters kept by Barnabas's mother. The pictures were traced from coloring books, working
on a window in the daytime or a piece of double-strength
glass (such as used for a tabletop) with a lamp beneath. The
other example is a simple stick-figure drawing.

Service and Social Sharing

To quickly involve a larger class or younger students
in creative Bible projects, set up interest centers, in which
members choose a table or corner by type of activity to be
done in small groups. Each center could have a colorful
poster inviting people to join it, or leaders could recruit
participants as they arrive. Set a maximum number at each
center so all students are somewhat evenly divided among
them.
    Save some time for sharing of the "products" (even if

Barnabas's real name is Joses (like mine). He was born in Cyprus and grew up there.

When he got big he liked to help people. He even helped Paul once

Then Uncle Bannie teached some people in a church in Antioch (later Paul came to help him)

After a while they were sent to be missionaries

. . . except for the time they had to go to Jerusalem for a big meeting

Finally Paul was ready for another trip but Uncle Barnie took John Mark and went to Cyprus.

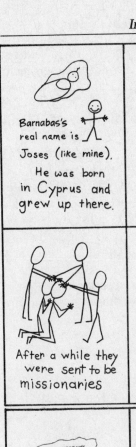

Acts 4:36

Acts 4:36-37

Acts 13 & 14

Barnabas & Paul on First Missionary Journey

Acts 13:50

Barnabas thrown out of Antioch in Pisidia for preaching Gospel.

Acts 14:1

Barnabas preaches to Jews in the Synagogues.

Acts 15:1-12

Barnabas at Jerusalem Council

Barnabas creative biographies

not all finished), as this will be a high time of fun and enthusiasm. Don't mind if groups don't finish their projects.
They may be so involved they'll want to stay later or meet
another time to continue them.

Each center leader must be enthusiastic and assume
his group will have fun getting involved.

Arrange for a "Jonah Night" (or use another Bible
book) as an evening service for the whole congregation. Get
pupils excitedly working toward this date as a motivational
goal to produce some good Bible projects. The idea is for
the Sunday school to take charge of the evening with everything done a by-product of their creative Bible activities.
Some of the elements of such a service could be:

- New words to sing to familiar hymn tunes
- Short individual presentations (messages, monolo-
  gues, paraphrases, or poetry)
- Group presentations (dialogues, drama vignettes, or
  pantomimes)
- Distribution of a Bible newspaper, crossword puzzle, or family game ideas
- Displays of posters, banners, and other student
  works

Such a service gives pupils a worthy goal beyond
themselves to work toward, brings joy to the adults present
at the service, and sets a beautiful model for younger ones
to follow.

Alternatives to a church service include guest teaching
for another age group (younger or older), program for an all-
church dinner, summer Bible school or missions projects,
or a social at which games and refreshments are all creative
Bible expressions. Each cupcake or cookie, for example,
could be decorated with a person, place, or event (symbol
or words) from the past quarter's lessons. As questions are
asked, correct answers may be eaten.

Ask the Lord which of these methods He would like
you to use with your class.

Joyfully involving students in Bible learning activities
will help you to be the best Sunday school teacher you can
be.

6

Dramatization: Getting Students Involved

Are you looking for teaching methods that can:

- Spark the interest of your class?
- Get your entire group actively involved?
- Generate lively discussion?
- Help students understand the viewpoints of others?
- Teach Bible customs in a hard-to-forget way?

Then you are looking for drama and role play.

Simply stated, role playing is an educational technique in which two or more members of the group act out a situation spontaneously. Drama usually requires a script, a larger cast, and more rehearsing. But technical distinctions between drama and role play grow fuzzy on the whole gamut in between.

To get a class actively involved with dramatization techniques, first and foremost determine your purpose. Why do you want your students to enact something? *Aims should always determine activities.*

Reinforce a Bible Story

Tell the Bible story as vividly as you can, asking each student to listen for which character he or she would like to portray.

After the story, help the class determine a brief sequence of scenes and characters. Try to get volunteers rather than assign parts. Be careful that an unpopular student doesn't end up with an unpopular role.

Suggest simple, general motions for students to act out parts. Old towels, sheets, robes and shirts make good costumes. Let imagination be the main props.

Divide older children into two or three groups, assigning a scene for each to dramatize. Warm up each player by asking questions about the character he will be portraying. A Bible quiz or drill could be included as part of the preparation process.

Imaginatively add humorous details to stories, such as the following. Before Babel the whole world spoke one language—English! (Or was it Swedish?) But one Tuesday morning Joe, working on the forty-ninth floor, called to Harry on forty-eight for more bricks. "Ach du lieber!" "Qu'est-ce que c'est?" The whole project ground to a halt when the workers couldn't communicate. God frustrated their rebellious efforts by twisting their tongues. People who could understand one another got together and moved off to start their own civilization.

For a new approach to a familiar Bible story, interview the main character(s) on the telephone, as Dan Zachary did with Noah.

> [SOUND: Dial tone, phone being dialed, two rings of phone]
> WIFE: Hello.
> INTERVIEWER: Is this Mrs. Noah?
> WIFE: Yes, it is.
> INTERVIEWER: Is Mr. Noah there? I'd like to speak to him.
> WIFE: Sure, I'll put him on.
> NOAH: Hello.
> INTERVIEWER: Hi. This is Dan Zachary in Chicago. I heard that you had quite an adventuresome boat ride a few years ago and would like to know more about it. I wonder if you could help me.
> NOAH: Be glad to if I can.
> INTERVIEWER: Thanks a lot. Before we talk

about the ride, could you give me a little background on your family? I'm writing a report for Sunday school, and anything you can tell me will be a big help.

NOAH: Well sure, Dan. I was born one thousand and fifty six years after Adam. Remember him? Adam and Eve?

INTERVIEWER: Sure. I've studied about them in Sunday school.

NOAH: My dad, Lamech, was about one hundred and eighty two at the time. Many of my ancestors were still alive. I got to meet all but Adam, Seth, and Enoch. Enoch walked with God, you remember. You can read our family tree in the book of Genesis. God did a great job in preserving it for you.

INTERVIEWER: I know. I'm glad that He did. How about the wife and kids?

NOAH: The Mrs. and I have been married for a long time, but we didn't have any children until after I was five hundred. And then we only had three.

INTERVIEWER: Let me guess. Two boys and a girl?

NOAH: No, all boys.

INTERVIEWER: What were their names?

NOAH: Shem, Ham, and Japheth. Ours was an unusual marriage for our time. Many people married young and then got divorced so they could remarry. Or they just had children without getting married. Needless to say, many of the homes were broken, and the kids weren't brought up right. I'm glad we waited until later and brought our children up right. As a young man I recognized that the way our neighbors were acting was not pleasing to God. I purposed in my heart to follow after God. . . .

Bridge Cultural Gaps

Flesh out the story, pooling suggestions as to how people and animals might have looked and acted. Children need imaginative details added to help strengthen their mental images. For example, a phrase such as the *wicked generation* needs to be translated into "men with shifting eyes, crouching over, sneaking around looking for trouble to get into, saying bad things behind people's backs."

Make your class feel like they are detectives looking for clues. A good resource to help you is *The Victor Handbook of Bible Knowledge* (Victor Books), which verbally and visually amplifies about three hundred of the Bible's major stories. Also helpful is a book on Bible customs such as Fred Wight's *Manners and Customs of Bible Lands* (Moody Press).

Where geography is important to the action, lay out an imaginary Bible map on the classroom floor, using individuals or objects to represent water bodies or cities.

A clever twist is to retell the story through the eyes of a minor character or an animal who might have been there. For example, eavesdrop on two sheep talking in a pasture outside the Jerusalem wall (by Ray Walters).

[SOUND: Hammering and chiseling on rocks]

YOUNG SHEEP: What's all that commotion going on for? Baa, baa.

OLD SHEEP: The priests and Eliashib are building the walls and the Sheep Gate.

YOUNG SHEEP: [inquisitively] How do you know?

OLD SHEEP: [speaking softly] Well, the other night while grazing in the grass along the Valley of Hinnom, I saw several men walking by the ruins. I got closer to them, and one man, who was on a donkey, began picking up rocks, writing something down on scrolls, and telling the others what to do and which way to go.

YOUNG SHEEP: [butting in] So what?

OLD SHEEP: Well, I followed them at a close distance all the way around the city almost to the Gihon Springs. However, they stopped (it seems the debris was too difficult to pass), and the fellow on the donkey got off, shaking his head. Then I heard him say, "It looks bad, but these walls and gates can be built! Together we can do it, and with God's guidance and our prayers, I'm just the man to get God's work done!" But at that moment the wind picked up, and I couldn't hear what they said. The clouds covered the moon, and they seemed to disappear into David's old palace. I did hear one last voice. Though I couldn't see anyone, the voice said, "Nehemiah, it's good you're coming here. Get the people interested, and they'll have a mind to work." Yes, I think this man from Persia is getting the people to build the city again.

YOUNG SHEEP: That's crazy. Baa-aaaaaa. They can never do it. It's just too much work.

OLD SHEEP: I don't know about that. Look at 'em. Why, all the priests for the first time in years seem to be doing something together. They're even working all the way to the Tower of Hananel.

YOUNG SHEEP: Can't be done. No way! Baa-aaa.

OLD SHEEP: Well, if they do, you and I will be in for real *trouble*.

YOUNG SHEEP: How's that?

OLD SHEEP: Well, since my ancestors' time of Zerubbabel I haven't seen or heard about so much activity. Any scholarly sheep knows that when the Jews start moving, God is moving. That means Temple worship again. That can only lead to one thing.

YOUNG SHEEP: [extremely curious] What's that?

OLD SHEEP: [sighing] Baaa-aaaaa. The altar.

YOUNG SHEEP: The altar! Will we be sacrifices? I don't like this Nehemiah! Ba-ba-ba-ba.

OLD SHEEP: Well, you're not the only one. I've heard rumors to the effect that a certain nearby governor (mind you, I'm not quoting any names) and his henchmen are plotting against Nehemiah. Seems they don't like him either.

YOUNG SHEEP: This scares me. I don't like to see all those men working so hard. And all this talk about sacrificing. No way!

OLD SHEEP: Face facts, son. Look at what our forefathers did when their blood was smeared over the lintels back in Egypt. Why, they saved the young boy babies of Israel from death. What do you think we're here for? Just to eat grass? Be thankful you would be chosen for a sacrifice to God.

YOUNG SHEEP: [speaking quickly] I'm going to Samaria! I'm getting out of here! Baaa-baaaa-baaaa!

Pose a Problem to Discuss

It might be a problem described in Scripture. For example, the two groups of women disputing the method of food distribution (Acts 6) could be enacted as an open-ended story, setting the stage for discussion of possible solutions.

Or it might be a modern problem situation. For example, involve the whole class in role playing a girl being made fun of at school by her peers because she is not dressed like them. Then ask probing questions, such as, "How would you have felt if you were the girl? What would you do if you were her best friend in class? What if you were a teacher observing this behavior?"

What biblical principles apply in this case? Groups could plan and present skits demonstrating the outworking of the lesson truth in modern life.

Read with Variety

Read Scripture aloud to babies and young children, using a simple Bible version or storybook. You may want to restate the narrative in your own words.

With older children and teens, vary between reading in unison, by parts, or responsively. Study a Bible portion, and mark it for different voice parts. Photocopy the passage and color-code it with felt-tip markers. Some parts could be read by all in unison for emphasis.

Ask the "who, what, when, where, why, and how" questions mentioned in chapter 1 to increase comprehension. Juniors or young teens enjoy being detectives looking for clues about the above topics.

Always go beyond the facts to life application by asking, "What does God want us to be or do?"

As you read a passage together, stop when someone spots a command, good example, or other application to us.

Have individuals research meanings and applications for key words encountered, using a Bible or English dictionary or whatever Bible study helps are available.

Discuss what emotions might have been felt by those in the passage. Help your students develop their ability to read with varying inflection to project both meaning and mood.

People of all ages will enjoy making a cassette tape of some Scripture. Photocopy the passage to mark portions for different readers. Younger ones can provide sound effects (crying, laughing, banging pan lids for thunder, splashing water, or stomping feet for travel).

Here's My Version

Most people like to read the Bible in a paraphrase—someone else's retelling of the Bible truths in simpler and more modern language. It's even more enjoyable to make up one's own Bible paraphrase.

For variety, consider the following approaches to paraphrasing: ☐ Simple language for children ☐ Street language for an inner-city gang ☐ Humorous for a skit night ☐ Ultra-contemporary for modern unchurched teens ☐ Serious for a senior citizens' service.

Here's how Cheri Strahm paraphrased Nehemiah 10, a passage that is only ancient history on the surface.

> 1 Now on the church covenant were the names of the pastor, Richard Rice, and the youth pastor, Richard Strahm; 2 Also John Bell, Bill Thompson, Norm Van Dersen, Neal Storm, and Harold DeVries. These were the church deacons.

9 And the trustees: Jim Hendrix, Bob Lindsey, John Whitman, and Harry Lachher. 14 And the Sunday school teachers: Phil Grossman, Dale McGuffy, Doris Lane, Polly Eireman, Bob Hobbs, Cheri Strahm, Bill Vanderguesen, Norm Thompsonn, Jerry Kingery, George Lane, Shirley Bell, and Edward Thompson. 28 Now the rest of the people signed, too: the choir members, young people, janitors, women's missionary fellowship, children's church, and all who had determined to live separate from the world in obedience to God; all the men, women, and children, by families, who were capable of understanding the extent and importance of such a commitment. 29 All of these signed a sworn statement, pledging the following: to walk according to the standards of God's Word, which was provided for us by more than forty men of God who wrote as directed by the Holy Ghost; to know and willingly obey the commands of our Lord, and all He has asked us to do in His Word; 30 To not be unequally yoked with those who shun the name of Christ, following only their own selfish pursuits; 31 To refuse to buy or sell any merchandise on the Lord's Day, thus keeping it as a day of rest; to take an occasional rest, too, from the rat-race business world, giving those we work with a break, and spending the extra time with the Lord and our families. 32 We also pledge to contribute annually a reasonable sum (at least a third of a day's wages) for the sole purpose of church maintenance and improvement; 33 For the purchase of a new church bus; for the cleaning of the carpets, baptismal, and windows; for the replacement of our old out-dated hymnals; and for all other necessities that pertain to the house of God. 34 Also we pledge to take turns, by families, in providing the Communion elements, which are an important part of our regular church worship; 35 And we pledge to bring money gifts to the Lord as He prospers us, Sun-

day by Sunday, as the fruit of our week's labor. 36 We will dedicate our sons, daughters, and business endeavors to the Lord, asking the pastor to pray with us in our commitment; 37 And in effect we will dedicate all areas of our lives to God, surrendering all for His use. We will support the pastor and church staff also and will not neglect their needs. 38 The pastor pledges to see to the needs of his deacons and other church leaders also, guiding them in their church duties and responsibilities. 39 And all the people, the deacons, trustees, church musicians, everyone, will not neglect to provide money, time, and talent to the church program; we will not neglect our attendance in the Lord's house.

You can make your own Bible version to read like *Pilgrim's Progress* by inserting the meaning of names where used. Look up proper Bible names in a Bible dictionary or unabridged concordance (such as Strong's). For example, *Terah*, Abraham's father, means "moon god." His nephew *Lot* means "a pebble" or a "small piece of wood." They originally lived in *Ur*, meaning "fire," and traveled to *Haran*, meaning "camel caravan route." Hence, part of Genesis 11 and 12 would read: "The exalted father took the moon god, the contentious one, and the pebble and left the flame to travel to the camel caravan route."

Let the group practice this technique on one of the Bible's family trees, such as in Matthew 1.

Show a Story

Every Sunday school needs visuals for Bible stories. Excellent flannelgraphs, filmstrips, flip charts, teaching pictures, and overhead transparencies are commercially available. I enjoy using those drawn by artist Bill Hovey (from Bill Hovey Visuals), whose rendition of Daniel appears on the next page.

Video cassette recorders (called VCRs) are easily connected to a television set or monitor and allow playback of prerecorded video programs whenever desired. Their pop-

Story of Daniel by Bill Hovey

ularity is enhanced by ease of operation.

Dramatized Bible stories can be rented for about the same cost as buying a book. Video cassettes with all their action keep all the advantages of a book. Index markers serve as table of contents and page numbers. Skimming is easy with a video player running at a faster-than-normal speed. But any "page" can be frozen for close scrutiny. Instant replay of any scene is the user's choice. Easy stopping and starting facilitate discussion and interaction with the program.

Have older students create visuals for use with younger ones. The story of Noah below was simply done freehand with felt-tip markers and construction paper by Priscilla Sebby.

Noah's story

Abraham's story scenes were originally made as dioramas (three-dimensional scenes) in boxes before photos were taken by Dan Genheimer. The base is a sweater, background is construction paper, and characters are blown-out eggshells with floral-wire bodies.

Abraham's story

Abraham, Lot, and Sarah
go to the land of Canaan.

Abraham rescues Lot
from captivity.

Abraham and Sarah are
visited by angels.

Abraham prepares to
sacrifice his son Isaac.

The "Turning TV" is a shoe box with a hole cut in the front and covered with cellophane by Mark Reed. Dials are drawn with a felt-tip pen. Two slender cans enable a picture roll to be progressively turned across the "screen." The story of Ezra in this example was drawn scene-by-scene on a long roll of paper.

The overhead projector can be an "enlarged flannelgraph with motion" by mounting silhouette figures and scenes on plastic sticks. Simply cut around figures printed on paper; the paper will block the projector light. Backing them with cardboard isn't necessary but gives more rigidity. A story like Jonah and the great fish works well this way. Have the fish with an open mouth and Jonah as a small figure. Children of all ages will be fascinated by the action. Some will be eager volunteers to manipulate the pieces.

Slide programs become far more interesting to stu-

The letter E

E is for Elephant.

E is for Eggs.

E is for Ezra.

What's an Ezra?

Ezra is a Bible book with three main characters.

Cyrus the King

Zerubbabel checks his roster of Hebrews who returned.

Cyrus gives official decree for Hebrews to return.

Hebrews rebuild the Temple and its altar.

dents and parents alike when the class is the cast. Draw up a list of the different scenes needed to tell the story. Then stage each one, snapping it as a still shot with a camera loaded with color slide film. For parts of the story difficult to reenact, simply take a slide of an appropriate picture from a Bible story book to intersperse with your live-actor photos. (Be sure to ask permission of the copyright holder.)

Elaborate costuming isn't necessary; imagination is a great substitute. To depict a prophet preaching to Israel, for example, take a close-up photo of one person standing with his mouth open and a hand outstretched, pointing one finger. A long shot of him and his audience (the rest of the class) sets the scene. Note one youth group's rendition of the book of Ezra on the next page.

Keep your purpose in mind so you can spot when it has been realized. Don't allow the dramatic activity to drag beyond the point of real value. Follow through immediately with some good discussion questions.

The Story of Ezra

God calls Zerubbabel to
rebuild the Temple

The foundation of God's
Temple is restored.

Samaritans temporarily
stop the work.

Ezra mourns over the
people's sin.

If your class time is too limited, plan a class social using fun student involvement techniques to review a past unit or lesson.

Involving students in in-class drama will help you to be the best Sunday school teacher you can be.

7

Retention: Making Memorizing a Joy

Like many things in life, memorizing Scripture is easier when working with someone else. The process will become more enjoyable as you follow this chapter's suggestions.

Use SWAP as an acrostic word to remember four methods of Scripture memory. SWAP means Say it aloud, Write it down, Act it out, and Pray it back (to God). Later we'll stutter on this acrostic, adding more Ps at the end.

Suggest we want to swap time for more of God's Word in our minds. Pick a verse or short passage to practice these techniques together. Use selections your group does not already know. Colossians 3:16 will be used as the main example.

Say It Aloud

To introduce Colossians 3:16, ask how many pupils know John 3:16. "Let's say it together." For a laugh, only recite the book and reference: "John 3:16." Then add, "I guess you all know it." Then recite together the words of the verse. Ask how many reviewed it today. (They just did.)

Stress that any part of God's Word can be as much at home in us (and recallable any time) if we'll give it the time and attention John 3:16 has gotten over the years. Make the memory link that we are about to learn another 3:16, this time in the book of Colossians.

To memorize the reference, recite book, chapter, and verse before and after the text.

Begin by reciting a phrase of the verse, making a "come here" gesture with your hand. This indicates that members should repeat in unison what you said.

When you ask a question about the Scripture portion without motioning, students should answer the question from the verse being learned. Holding both hands out as though you were indicating the length of something means students should recite the verse from the beginning.

Now proceed in a rapid-fire manner with a random barrage of the signals, being careful not to push your pupils beyond their abilities. But don't make it too easy, or they'll lose interest. Of course, your biggest challenge might be keeping the signals straight yourself.

Read Colossians 3:16 aloud together from a displayed copy: "Colossians 3:16, 'Let the word of Christ dwell in you richly in all wisdom, teaching and admonishing one another with psalms and hymns and spiritual songs, singing with grace in your hearts to the Lord,' Colossians 3:16"

> Teacher: "Let" (sweeping motion)
> Students: "Let"
> Teacher: "the word of Christ" (sweeping
>   motion)
> Students: "the word of Christ"
> Teacher: (parenthesis motion)
> Students: "Let the word of Christ"
> Teacher: "What is the first word of this verse?"
> Students: "Let"
> Teacher: "Whose word are we talking about?"
> Students: "Christ's"
> Teacher: "What is it that belongs to Christ this
>   verse speaks of?"
> Students: "the word"
> Teacher: "dwell in you" (sweeping motion)
> Students: "dwell in you"
> Teacher: (parenthesis motion)
> Students: "Let the word of Christ dwell in you"
> Teacher: "Where should the word of Christ be?"
> Students: "in you"

Teacher: "What should it be doing in there?"
Students: "dwelling"

As they catch the concept, go faster and try to mix them up between the two hand signs and questions you ask. Drop in an occasional unrelated surprise question ("How old are you?" or, "Who's your best friend?").

Work in pairs to see who can learn the rest of the verse first. Only the older student should look at the words while he pumps the passage into the younger one. Then review the entire verse as a class.

Write It Down

Put the selected verse on the board or a transparency so all are learning the same verse in the same version for practice. Have each work individually to copy the verse, fold his paper over what he copied, and try to write it from memory. Correct mistakes and blanks, trying again, continuing this procedure until each can write the whole verse easily from memory.

Review the memory verse by writing the first letter of each word. When a verse has more than one sentence or thought, it helps to write each segment on a separate line. Here's how Colossians 3:16 looks:

L TW0 C D I Y R I AW
T A A0 A I P A H A S S
SW G I Y H T T L.
C 3 1 6

Make review posters or transparencies, leaving scattered words out of the verse. Have students recite only the missing words as you point to them. For example:

"Colossians 3:16, 'Let __ word __ Christ dwell __ __ rich-ly __ __ wisdom, teaching __ admonishing __ another __ psalms __ hymns __ _____ songs, singing __ grace __ ____ hearts __ __ Lord,' Colossians 3:16."

Or:

"Colossians 3:16, '__ the word of Christ ____ in you ____ in all wisdom, _____ and _____ one another in psalms and hymns and spiritual songs, ____ with grace in your hearts to the Lord,' Colossians 3:16."

When the group thinks they know the verse, use this quiz:

"Colossians __:__, '__ __ ____ _ _____ _____ __ __ ____ __ __ _____, _____ ___ _____ __ _____ __ _____ __ ____ __ _____ _____, _____ __ ____ __ ___ _____ __ __ ____,' Colossians __:__."

For fun, ask someone who "knows it all" to spell the verse. For a social or presession review activity, replace each letter with a blank line to play the popular pencil-and-paper game "hangman."

Give or have each student write on an index card the words of Colossians 3:16 on one side and its reference on the other. Encourage each to carry the card during the week to practice while waiting, walking, or doing other routine activities. Tape a copy of the verse to the bathroom mirror or some other place where it can be seen regularly. Ask the Lord to help members obey His command to hide His word in their hearts (Psalm 119:9-11 and Colossians 3:16).

Act It Out

Ask how many know the words and hand motions to the children's rhyme, "Here's the church, here's the steeple; open the doors, and see all the people." Do it (with motions) together. Make a funny comment like, "Isn't that cute?" or, "You should see yourselves." Ask how many haven't done that for at least five years. Yet they still remember it, illustrating the value of adding motions with the words of verses as a personal memory crutch. Demonstrate a verse you have learned this way or the Zephaniah 3:17 sample below.

"Zephaniah 3:17, 'The Lord your God [point up with four choppy motions for the four words] is with you [wave out across the group], He is mighty [flex bicep] to save [form a cross with two fingers]. He [point to heaven] will take great delight [smile broadly as you wave both hands raised straight up] in you [point to someone in group], He [point up] will quiet [finger to mouth like "shhh"] you [point at someone] with His love [hug yourself with both arms], He [point up] will rejoice [use both fingers to draw a happy face on yourself] with singing [wave like songleading],' Zephaniah 3:17 [NIV]."

After students make up motions as pairs to Colossians 3:16, have pairs demonstrate. If they are inhibited, demonstrate as a group in unison (or by halves of the big group).

After motions have been learned, do motions together as a whole class *silently* (each member making his motions, but thinking of the words only).

Pray It Back

List the three ways to turn Scripture into prayer using the acrostic THI (Thank You, Help me, I confess). Demonstrate with Zephaniah 3:17. Emphasize it should be a personal, first-person version of the verse. Let small groups practice doing this with Colossians 3:16. Don't force anyone to pray, as some might be inhibited about praying out loud in a group. Let it be voluntary conversational-style prayer. Emphasize that no group should just "pray around the circle."

Ponder Its Meaning

By stuttering on the acrostic SWAPPP, we can add two Ps for other memory helps: Ponder Its Meaning and Picture It.

Recite Colossians 3:16 several times, emphasizing a different word each time. For example, "*Let* the word of Christ dwell in you richly . . ." "Let *the word* of Christ dwell in you richly . . ." "Let the word *of Christ* dwell in you richly . . ." "Let the word of Christ *dwell* in you richly . . ." "Let the word of Christ dwell *in you* richly . . ." "Let the word of Christ dwell in you *richly . . .*"

Briefly discuss the meaning or significance of each emphasized word. Consult a Bible dictionary for help in understanding people, places, and perplexing terms. A regular English dictionary will also help explain unfamiliar words.

An exhaustive concordance, like Strong's or Young's, defines every word in the Bible from its original language. You may also want to get a reliable Bible commentary to understand words and phrases in their contexts. (For help in using Bible study tools, consult chapters 7 and 8 of *Off the Shelf and into Yourself,* published by Victor Books.)

Look up information about the book of Colossians and its author in a Bible dictionary.

Then read Colossians; it's only three chapters long.

Summarize how the historical setting helps us understand the verse we are learning. As a group, answer these questions:

• To whom was this book written?
• What news did the author have to deliver?
• How might the original readers have felt after reading or hearing this letter for the first time?
• How do the verses surrounding 3:16 contribute to our understanding of it? (It's in a lengthy list of commands from God to us. We'll be more likely to obey the surrounding commands if we have Christ's words and His wisdom in our hearts.)
• What special encouragement can we find in Colossians 3:16?

Picture It

Have each member draw doodles for each word or phrase in the memory verse. Here are some examples from part of Zephaniah 3:17 (NIV)—"The Lord your God [draw a triangle labeled T.L.Y.G.] is with you [draw stick figures around your triangle], He is mighty [draw a man's flexed bicep] to save [draw a cross]."

Using only one of the above memory techniques each

week gives seven ways to relearn a verse without seeming to be repetitious.

Develop a class plan for Bible memorization, deciding how much you want to have learned by a specific date. Then break the goal into bite-sized pieces.

For example, to learn ten verses related to salvation during a ten-week period, memorize one verse each week. For a small book like Philippians, learning only two verses a week means memorizing the entire book in a year. Some memorize continuous passages without the verse numbers.

Many people consider one or two verses a week a good, steady diet. Ask the Lord to show you together how much Scripture He wants your class to memorize. Encourage members to depend on the Holy Spirit daily to give discipline and remembrance.

Some Teaching Tips

Write the verse to be learned on a big posterboard with key words stuck on different colored shapes with Velcro. When a word is removed, the shape and color remain where the word was. Have younger volunteers take a word off, asking what word was removed. Or letter the verse on an overhead transparency sheet for quick display and removal.

If an older group needs extra motivation to memorize, quote an extended passage of Scripture you have committed to memory and testify of the personal value you have found in doing this.

Or ask, "Are you happy with your thought life? Do you ever wonder why you say or think some of the things you do? Would you like to more and more be able to automatically respond as God would have you to?" These are some of the benefits we can experience for regular, systematic Scripture memory and meditation. God's Word can cleanse and reprogram our mental computers.

Read Ecclesiastes 4:9-12 together. Brainstorm other examples of the two-are-better-than-one principle. Have members commit their Bible memory goals to the Lord and to a human partner. Have the partners agree to pray for and creatively encourage each other as many ways as possible during the next week (or twenty-one days). Suggest they call each other unexpectedly with a word of encouragement or to hear the portion learned thus far. Remind teens to call their partners at a reasonable hour.

For older members who are discouraged with their abilities, state there are only three hindrances to memorizing this way in class together: pride, lack of motivation, and an evil heart of unbelief. The latter does not believe God's power can help us memorize. Intelligence is not a factor. You can assure students if they have enough intelligence to dress and feed themselves, they have enough to obey God's command to memorize Scripture.

Memory is unsanforized, subject to shrinkage unless we review. If we relearn a verse daily for twenty-one days, we will probably be able to say it easily. Recite or read Philippians 4:13 together as encouragement.

In my early teaching days, I would tell my students what to learn, send them out to learn it, then check on them later. I was just a dispenser and checker of truth, not a teacher. We haven't taught unless pupils have learned. If it's worth learning, we learn it on the spot together. I now guarantee my students that if they are alive, alert, and attending, we will memorize in class together 100 percent of what I want them to recall. They won't have to learn it outside of class—just review it.

Memorizing Scripture alone and with students will help you to be the best Sunday school teacher you can be.

8

Imagination: Learning Lists Easily

Do you ever want your students to remember lists from the Bible, such as the Twelve Apostles or the Ten Commandments? It's possible to teach lists so students have a hard time forgetting them.

Such lists may be recalled in or out of sequence. For example, what is the fifth commandment? Or which one deals with adultery? Such questions are easy to answer if lists have been learned with mental pictures.

Use the memory techniques in this chapter for Bible lists, sessions in a quarter's study, and where to find subjects in Bible books.

Ten Great Commands

Could you name the Ten Commandments in the order God gave them? See what sense you can make of the symbols below as a memory device.

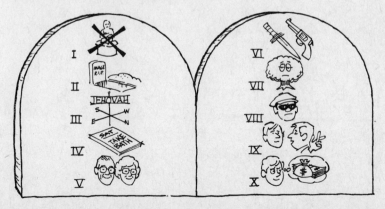

Here's the key:

1. No other gods
2. No graven images
3. No vain (vane?) use of God's name
4. Keep the Sabbath day
5. Honor your parents

6. No killing
7. No adultery (a dull tree?)
8. No stealing
9. No bearing false witness
10. No coveting

Have your students practice describing the ten pictures in order without looking at them. After some partner or group drilling on each picture's meaning, quiz the group orally on their ability to list the Ten Commandments, both in and out of sequence.

Stack Them Up

Show a picture like the one below, and ask the more intelligent one to explain it to his partner.

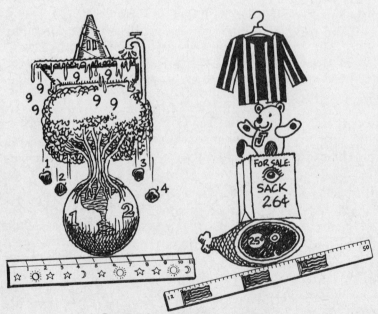

Genesis memory stack

The rest of this section is suggested wording when using this picture. Make a transparency of the picture or copies for each student.

This picture is the book of Genesis. This is my crazy way to remember the big ideas in order and teach them to others. On this picture are stacked twenty specific pieces of factual information: Two major divisions of Genesis and what chapters are in them; eight subdivisions of the book and chapters for each.

The bottom ruler has how many units? (11) What are its symbols? (sun, moon, stars) Could we not then call this a *universal* ruler? In Genesis 1-11 we have the universal rule of God over all creation (the Hebrews are not singled out yet).

How many units are on the second ruler? (50) What are the symbols? (flags) This is the *national* rule of God over the Hebrews. Each of the rulers is a big division of Genesis.

Each ruler has four sub-parts. Note the globe. How many hemispheres are depicted? (2) How many chapters of Genesis are about the creation? (first 2) How many apples are *falling* from the tree? (4) So through chapter 4 is the fall into sin. (I often jokingly add that the forbidden tree in Eden must have borne apples, pears, or oranges because those are the only three tempting to me. Who would plunge the world into sin for a bite of kumquat?)

What's wrong with the bathtub? (water running over) What number are the water drops forming? (9) So through chapter 9 is the Flood. In the tub is a floating tower with how many windows? (2) But what number do the windows form? (11) So through chapter 11 is the Tower of Babel.

Notice the numbers are always for the upper limits of the section. So what are the chapter limits for each symbol? (Universal rule of God, 1-11; Creation, 1-2; Fall, 3-4; Flood, 5-9; Tower of Babel, 10-11)

What seems about to roll off the second ruler? (a ham) What is its sale price? (.25) Who is the big *ham* of Genesis 12-25? (Abraham) What's in the sack? (eyes) Guess why we call that an eye-sack (Isaac). How many eyes are in the sack? (26) Here is a 36-year old J-cub (Jacob). Who had a coat of many colors (last symbol)? (Joseph)

Review the second section by questions.

Suggest students choose carefully what they look at and what they say, because that's what they'll remember. Later go back through the images stack, pretending to point to them on the front wall or on the blank screen (picture not displayed) and ask: □ How many rulers were there? □ What was on them? □ What do these symbols stand for? □ How many units on each? □ What was about to roll off the bottom ruler? □ How many hemispheres were depicted? □ What was growing out of the globe? (And so on through the stack)

It works just as well to ask members to use their imaginations. A displayed picture is not necessary to learn lists with memory stacks.

Sing the following song, which uses the hymn tune, "O Zion, Haste," to recall the same information as the Genesis memory picture.

Putting Books in Order

Can you and your students name the 39 Old Testament books in order? If not, orally drill with the following form until your students can recite them all. Make one copy of the form with only blank boxes for members to look at and another with books named as below.

The Topical Old Testament

5	5	5
Genesis	Job	Isaiah
Exodus	Psalms	Jeremiah
Leviticus	Proverbs	Lamentations
Numbers	Ecclesiastes	Ezekiel
Deuteronomy	Song of Solomon	Daniel

9		9
Joshua		Hosea
Judges		Joel
Ruth		Amos
1 Samuel		Obadiah
2 Samuel		Jonah
1 Kings		Micah
2 Kings		Nahum
1 Chronicles		Habakkuk
2 Chronicles		Zephaniah

3		3
Ezra		Haggai
Nehemiah		Zechariah
Esther		Malachi

It's easier to learn them by their small subgroups of 5, 9, or 3, then put the small groups together.

Here are the 39 Old Testament books set to music in their topical groupings. The tune is "Did You Ever See a Lassie?" You'll have to tamper a bit with the notes to make some of the words fit.

Most students know the five books of Moses (Genesis through Deuteronomy), but need help thereafter. The twelve history books can be recalled by singing *J J R, 2 S K C; after them come E N E* to the tune of "Twinkle, Twinkle Little Star." These remind us of Joshua, Judges, Ruth, and

Books of the Old Testament

1. Let us sing the books of Mo-ses, of Mo-ses, of Mo-ses. Let us sing the books of
2. Let us sing the books of his-try, of his-try, of his-try. Let us sing the books of
3. Let us sing the books of poe-try, of poe-try, of poe-try. Let us sing the books of
4. Let us sing the ma-jor pro-phets, the pro-phets, the pro-phets. Let us sing the ma-jor
5. Let us sing the mi-nor pro-phets, the pro-phets, the pro-phets. Let us sing the mi-nor

Mo-ses, of which there are five. Gen-e-sis, Ex-o-dus, then
his-try, of which there are twelve. Josh-u-a, and Jud-ges, the
The Chron-i-cles fol-low, then
poe-try, of which there are five. Job, Psalms, and the Pro-verbs, and
pro-phets, of which there are five. Is-a-iah, Jer-e-mi-ah who
pro-phets, of which there are twelve. Ho-se-a, and Jo-el, and
Ha-bak-kuk, Zeph-a-ni-ah,

comes Le-vi-ti-cus. Num-bers, Deu-ter-on-o-my, that is the law.
sto-ry of Ru-th— First and Sec-ond Sam-u-el, then come the Kings.
Ez-ra the scri-be— then comes Ne-he-mi-ah and Es-ther the queen.
then Ec-cle-si-as-tes. Sol-o-mon's song fol-lows to close this sec-tion.
wrote Lam-en-ta-tions. E-zek-iel and Dan-iel, both true to their God.
Am-os the shep-herd. O-bad-i-ah, Jo-nah, Mi-cah, and Na-hum.
And there was Hag-ga-i, Ze-char-i-ah, and Mal-a-chi at the end.

Adapted from *Bible Panorama,* © Victor Books, 1985.

books each of Samuel, Kings, and Chronicles. Are there any more history books? Yes, *E N E* (sounds like *any*) helps us remember Ezra, Nehemiah, and Esther.

Recall that Israel and Judah were *L E D* by prophets to remember the five major prophets: Isaiah, Jeremiah, Lamentations, Ezekiel, and Daniel.

For the twelve minor prophets, pull off the first two letters of each, and recite them as three lines of poetry:

Ho Jo Am
Ob Jo Mi Na
Ha Ze Ha Ze Ma

Note the lines have three, four, and five syllables as we proceed down. Sing the round, say the poem, and review the Old Testament books several times out loud, and it'll be difficult to forget them in Bible order.

Build on What They Know

Note how much easier it is to learn the following twenty-six names and titles of Jesus because they are arranged on our familiar English alphabet.

Alpha (Revelation 21:6)
Bread of Life (John 6:35)
Carpenter (Mark 6:3)
Door (John 10:2)
Eternal Father (Isaiah 9:6)
Faithful One (Revelation 19:11)
Good Shepherd (John 10:11)
Holy One of God (Luke 4:34)
Immanuel (Matthew 1:23)
Jesus (Luke 1:31)
King of the Jews (Matthew 27:37)
Light of the World (John 9:5)
Messiah (John 4:25, 26)
Nazarene (Matthew 2:23)
Omega (Revelation 21:6)
Prince of Peace (Isaiah 9:6)

Quickener (Ephesians 2:1, 2)
Resurrection (John 11:25)
Savior (Luke 2:11)
Truth (John 14:6)
Unblemished Lamb (1Peter 1:19)
Vine (John 15:1)
Word (John 1:1)
X = abbreviation for "Christ" (first letter of Christ in Greek)
Yesterday the same (Hebrews 13:8)
Z = same as Omega (last letter of an alphabet)

Memory Pegs

Once learned, the ten pictures described below can be used for the remainder of one's life for any list to be learned.

Choose a rhyming word for each number.

One—run
Two—zoo
Three—tree
Four—door
Five—hive
Six—sick
Seven—heaven
Eight—gate
Nine—vine
Ten—hen

Ask questions like these: Which number rhymes with door? With vine? With a tree? Zoo? What is number four? Look at a list of numbers and think of all the rhymes. Look at a jumbled list of rhymes and think of their corresponding numbers. Say the list backwards with eyes closed.

Associate whatever is to be remembered with the corresponding memory picture. The first item is running, the second is in a zoo, and so on. Stress that each person must imagine the images in his mind for the method to work. Memory pegs may work better with children and teens at first because they can think of the images more easily than adults.

We could use the method as above, simple as it is. But it's even better to have a standard precise picture for each number which never changes except for the one new thing to be remembered.

- One—run: Imagine a horse *running* through the woods. Always put the item to be remembered in the saddle.
- Two—zoo: Picture the funniest creatures at the zoo (next to the people): monkeys hanging on their cages throwing the item to be remembered at the people.
- Three—tree: Picture a beautifully decorated Christmas *tree* on which the top ornament is always the item to be remembered.
- Four—door: Picture the item to be remembered stuck in a revolving *door*, making it impassable.
- Five—hive: Picture the item to be remembered flying around a *beehive*.
- Six—sick: Imagine you are approaching the item to be remembered in bed because it is *sick* and you are about to give it a hypodermic shot of medicine.
- Seven—heaven: Picture the item to be remembered going up and down a ladder into *heaven* (sky).
- Eight—gate: Picture the item to be remembered hanging on a railroad crossing *gate* flashing in place of the red lights.
- Nine—vine: Picture the item to be remembered hanging in clusters on a *grapevine*.
- Ten—hen: Picture a mother *hen* sitting on the item to be remembered as though it were eggs about to be hatched.

It sounds crazy, doesn't it? But it works. Sometimes the zanier the picture, the easier it is to remember. The method works even better if students make up their own rhyming words and standard memory pictures.

I have made and learned rhyming pegs through number 20. Thereafter, I imagine *two* identical horses for 21, *two* identical monkeys for 22. *Three* identical revolving doors would be 34, and so on.

After quizzing on the pictures, practice on a list of

items. The object is for each member to mentally visualize
the item to be remembered in the standard picture.

- One: a dove, a beautiful white bird. Where must you
  see the dove? (in the running horse's saddle)
- Two: a pair of trousers, Levi brand. Can you see the
  monkeys throwing them out of their cages? Once
  you see the image, let it go. It's only necessary to
  conjure up the image briefly.
- Three: a hand with its thumb pointing down. Looks
  crazy in your living room on the Christmas tree,
  doesn't it?

Review: What was in the saddle? What were the monkeys throwing? What was the picture for three? What was
the top ornament?

- Four: two bulls fighting. Can you see them blocking
  the revolving door?
- Five: pigs. They'll never make it inside the hive, but
  do you see them flying around its outside?
- Six: a big fish cooked and ready to eat. See it in the
  bed?
- Seven: a ferris wheel rolling up and down the ladder.

Review: One is run; what was in the horse's saddle?
Two is zoo; what were the monkeys throwing? Three is
tree; what was on top? Four is door; what kept it from revolving? Five is hive; what was flying around? Six is sick:
what was about to receive your hypo? Seven is heaven;
what was on the ladder?

- Eight: a loaf of bread, hanging and flashing on the
  gate.
- Nine: a white shirt glistening in the sun. See clusters
  of them hanging on the vine.
- Ten: a great amount of paper money. See the hen
  about to hatch the bundles of bills.

If you can see the mental memory pictures, you are

successful. Ask your students how well they know the first ten chapters of the gospel of Mark. Have them answer aloud with a number from 1 through 9 to each question below. In which chapter of Mark would you find: □ Pharisees bringing hard questions to Jesus? □ Jesus feeding 5,000? □ Feeding 4,000? □ Parables of the kingdom (sower and soils, etc.)? □ Transfiguration of Jesus? □ Jesus' baptism? □ Jewish leaders rejecting Jesus as Messiah?

Ask, "How did you do? You know more than you know you know. You can answer all of the above questions without realizing it."

When Jesus was baptized, in what form did the Holy Spirit come on Him? (Yes, a dove) Where was *dove* in our memory list? (1) When Jesus called Matthew the publican, what was this tax collector's other name? (Levi) Where was he in our list? Make a fist with your thumb pointing down, saying, "If this represents the Jewish leaders rejecting Jesus, thinking His power was from below, in what chapter of Mark do you think we'd find it?" (3) In which chapter do you think you'd find the "pair of bulls" (parables) about the kingdom of God? (4) When Jesus healed the Gadarene demoniac, where did the demons go after leaving the man? (into a herd of pigs) Therefore this incident must be in what chapter? (5) For fun, mention that this was the first recorded case of swine flu (flew). Let the fish remind us of Jesus feeding the 5,000 in chapter 6 by multiplying them. Could *ferris wheel* help remind us of Pharisees, who plied Jesus with loaded questions? If we let the *bread* (second letter of our alphabet) remind us of the second time Jesus fed a great multitude multiplying the loaves, what chapter? (8) When Jesus was transfigured, how did His clothes change in appearance? (They gleamed whiter than light.) Chapter? (9) Who went away from Jesus sorrowful because he had great possessions? (rich young ruler) In what chapter of Mark is he? (10)

Review. What chapter has Matthew, or Levi, called? (2, zoo) *Pharisees* giving Jesus static? (7, heaven) Jesus multiplying the bread for the second great miracle of feeding 4,000? (8, gate) Transfiguration of Jesus? (9, vine) Parables of the kingdom? (4, door)

Challenge students to practice with memory pegs for the Ten Commandments (listed in summary at the beginning of this chapter).

Using mental memory pictures will help you to be the best Sunday school teacher you can be.

9

Application: Fitting Life to Truth

Revelation demands a response. Scripture was given not just to satisfy our curiosity but to change our lives. If we aim for a life response, we're more likely to hit it.

Don't give students spiritual indigestion by stopping with the facts of Scripture. To make a difference in our lives, God's word needs to work in three areas: our minds, emotions, and wills. Ask, "What do I want my pupils to know, feel, and do as a result of this lesson?" Don't leave pupils the same. Take them from where they are to some new goal in life.

From a displayed or projected copy, recite together this statement several times, "We don't just read the Bible—we live it!" ("Study," "memorize," or "hear" may be substituted for "read.") Each time encourage more emphasis and decibels. Run a quick contest between two sides. Then let pupils try to forget that significant statement!

Here are several options to help students (and teachers) discover what God expects from them.

Sorting Out

One meaningful way to find personal application is to sort out God's responsibilities from ours.

Begin by drawing two vertical lines on a chalkboard or transparency, dividing it into three columns. Title the left column "My Duties" and the right "God's Duties." The middle column will be labeled "Results."

Choose one or more of the verses below, and guide students to divide each part of the verse into the three columns. Not every verse will contain information for all three.

My Duties	Results	God's Duties
John 3:16 Believe in God's Son	1. I won't perish 2. I'll have eternal life	1. Love the world 2. Give His only Son
1 Peter 2:2 Long for the pure milk of the Word like a newborn baby	I'll grow in respect to salvation	
Psalm 1:2-3 1. Delight in the law of the Lord 2. Meditate on His law day and night	1. I'll be like a tree firmly planted by streams of water 2. I'll yield fruit in season 3. My leaf won't wither 4. I'll prosper in whatever I do	

Have older students rule a sheet of paper into the above three columns and practice dividing a few verses. Using Psalm 119:1-8 or Philippians 4:4-9, work individually or in pairs.

Ask each to write down one thing he plans to do from his assigned responsibilities. After the chosen item, he should write out two or three specific action steps to accomplish it. Action steps for "keep my way pure," for example, might be: Stop reading a certain magazine; walk away from groups telling off-color stories; or, when lustful thoughts come, thank God for making girls.

Use what has been written into the three columns as a basis for conversational prayer. Ask God to help us carry out our specific duties, and thank Him for the results and for fulfilling His responsibilities.

Personalize God's Letters

Turn a Bible passage into a first-person prayer. For example, read James 1:1-8 (NIV):

> James, a servant of God and of the Lord Jesus Christ, to the twelve tribes scattered among the nations: Greetings. Consider it pure joy, my brothers, whenever you face trials of many kinds, because you know that the testing of your faith develops perseverance. Perseverance must finish its work so that you may be mature and complete, not lacking anything. If any of you lacks wisdom, he should ask God, who gives generously to all without finding fault, and it will be given him. But when he asks, he must believe and not doubt, because he who doubts is like a wave of the sea, blown and tossed by the wind. That man should not think he will receive anything from the Lord; he is a double-minded man, unstable in all he does.

Now compare this first-person prayer to the above passage.

> Father, I thank You that James was Your servant as well as the servant of the Lord Jesus Christ. Thank You for using James to send greetings to the twelve dispersed tribes. Lord, I also want to be known as one of Your servants. Please help me to bring Your good news to other people.
>
> When I face trials of many kinds, help me to consider it pure joy. Help me to realize in such times that the testing of my faith develops perse-

verance. Please help me to let perseverance finish its work so I may be mature and complete, not lacking anything.

Dear Father, when I lack wisdom, remind me to ask You. Thank You that You give generously to me without finding fault. Please help me to believe and not doubt when I ask You for help and wisdom with my problems and decisions. I don't want to be like a wave of the sea, blown and tossed by the wind. I want to receive what I ask from You. I don't want to be a double-minded person who is unstable in all he does.

In the name of Jesus. Amen.

Note how restating God's Word as a personal prayer brings its truths out of the ancient world right into our lives.

Stress that the prayer should be first-person whenever possible, using sanctified common sense as to what can be personally assumed. This technique presupposes we look at a passage for its life principles.

Personalized prayer works well on passages we have memorized, but we can also convert passages into such prayers as a meaningful method of Bible reading. Any part of the Bible can become a prayer book by reading it to the Lord and thanking Him for recording it. Thank Him individually for those mentioned in lists of names. Ask His help in carrying out our responsibilities.

Practice turning a portion of the Bible into a personal prayer, continuing with James 1 (start with verse 9) or using another passage.

Specs to See Better

Have your students read a Scripture portion and make notes on a sheet of paper with the five letters SPECS (an acrostic explaining five things to look for in a Bible passage) spaced vertically down the left side. We'll use Philippians 4 as an example.

Sins are attitudes or actions that displease the Lord

and should be forsaken. None are directly stated in Philippians 4:4-9. (Some categories don't apply to every Bible chapter.)

Promises are assurances or benefits from God to be claimed, but there are often conditions attached. The Lord is near (v. 5). God's peace surpasses all comprehension and will guard our hearts and minds in Christ Jesus (v. 7), but we must avoid being anxious by praying (v. 6). The God of peace will be with us (v. 9), but we have to practice Paul's commands in this portion of Scripture.

Examples are good attitudes or actions to imitate. Bad ones would be listed as sins or stumbling blocks. Have a positive outlook like Paul's in Philippians 4:4-9.

Commands are directions from God to obey. Rejoice in the Lord always (v. 4). Let your forbearing spirit be evident (v. 5). Let your requests be made known to God (v. 6). Think on things that are true, honorable, and so on (v. 8). Practice what we have learned from Paul (v. 9).

Stumbling blocks are things God warns us to avoid. Don't be anxious (v. 6).

Decide on one specific action to put into practice from this passage.

Dear Me

Distribute an envelope, stationery, and postage stamp to each member to write a letter to himself about what this quarter's study (or a particular Bible portion) has meant to him, what he wants to change in his life as a result, and how he plans to pursue this new goal.

Older students may want to scatter about the room or building for a specified time to be assured of privacy. Encourage reference to Bibles, texts, or notes during the writing.

When collecting the self-addressed, stamped, sealed letters, assure writers you won't peek, but will mail them in about six months.

Optionally write to a Bible author, expressing gratitude for his writing, asking any questions, and stating how his writing has affected our lives.

Or write a letter to God as suggested in chapter 1. Thank Him for what He has written and for what He has done, is doing, and has promised to do. Specifically ask His help to live the Christian life, admitting any sins or short-comings His Word has pointed out. Allow time for each to actually send (pray silently) his letter to God.

True or False?

Help your pupils create a true-false quiz from a Bible passage, each asking if what God says is true of him or not. Here are some sample true-false questions from James 1:1-8.

- Am I a servant of God?
- Am I a servant of the Lord Jesus Christ?
- Do I ever give God's greetings to others?
- Do I face trials of many kinds?
- Do I consider it pure joy when I face them?
- Do I know that the testing of my faith develops perseverance?
- Am I becoming mature and complete through perseverance?
- When I lack wisdom, do I first turn to God?
- Do I view God as One Who gives to me generously without finding fault?
- When I ask God for wisdom, do I ask doubting or believing?
- Am I double-minded and unstable in my ways?

Basic Principles

Ask what lessons for life God teaches through this week's Bible story or portion. Principles are like the "moral of the story" and may be directly stated or strongly implied.

The more historical the passage (relating events), the more principles are implied. The more doctrinal the passage (relating ideas), the more principles are explicitly stated.

We can't find an exact quotation of an implied principle because it's woven in as an underlying theme. When we see an implied principle, we are on good ground if we find that idea clearly taught in two or three different Bible passages. Consult the cross-references printed in many Bibles or look in a topical Bible such as Nave's *Topical Bible* (Moody Press), an index to Bible subjects.

Looking for principles in the Bible makes ancient passages seem more relevant. Practice looking for principles in Genesis 24 about how to be successful in dating or engagement. Here are a few examples to get started. There are many others.

- God must be the One to select our future mate (v. 7).
- Stake your marriage and happiness on God's reputation (v. 12).
- Set up guidelines for the ideal future mate (v. 14).
- Consult both sets of parents before making marriage plans (vv. 33-34).
- Establish financial responsibility to the potential in-laws (v. 36).
- Share the standards you've set for a future mate with the potential in-laws (v. 37).
- Honestly give the parents a choice regarding your potential mate (v. 49).
- Unity with parents and family is essential for a happy, successful engagement and/or marriage (vv. 51-58).

Get Specific

Generalities are a refuge for escape from real-life response. It's easy to get a class excited about being better Christians this week, but where do they start? How will they know if they are doing it right?

Don't assume anything when it comes to application of truth to life. Our lesson goal is not met if each student leaves knowing only a memory verse or central thought of a Bible text. Each must also know something specific God wants him to do as a result of exposure to His Word.

Christian teaching is a dynamic cooperation with God. The same Holy Spirit who indwells the teacher indwells every Christian student and convicts every nonbelieving one. The Holy Spirit of God is the great Motivator. Christian students leave our classroom with the Teacher living within them.

As teachers, we prepare, pray, and teach, but God is the only One who can effect life change. Pray for your pupils individually through the week, asking the Holy Spirit to motivate them to alter their lives to fit His Word.

Following our Lord's example, teaching for life response will help you to be the best Sunday school teacher you can be.

10

Visualization: Seeing What's Said

What do trees, money, pearls, sheep, wheat, hidden treasures, and mustard seeds have in common? Jesus used them all as audio or visual aids to help His disciples understand the mysteries of the kingdom of heaven. The Master Teacher often used concrete objects to communicate abstract spiritual truths.

There are many compelling reasons to use audio and visual aids.

If we could secure a videotape of our students' thoughts while we are teaching, what do you think we'd see? Not only do students' minds tend to wander, but attention spans are usually short. One study found that the average person spends 34 percent of a class hour looking around the room. What are we providing in our teaching environment to capture attention for our subject in each session?

Many teachers could correctly say to their classes, "I know you believe you understand what you think I said, but I'm not sure you realize that what you heard is not what I meant."

Communication breakdown is easily illustrated by asking children to draw their rendition of audio input. One child sketched a car with three occupants coming out of a cornfield after hearing about Adam and Eve being "driven" out of the Garden. Another drew an airplane to visualize "Pontius the pilot" taking Joseph, Mary, and the baby Jesus on the "flight" to Egypt.

Language barriers exist between teacher and student because each brings his own connotations to every concept. Imagine two worlds coming together and slightly overlapping. If one globe is the teacher and the other is the student, the small overlap is the area of meaning they hold in common.

What would your younger scholars visualize, for example, upon hearing about Elijah's throwing his *mantle* down to Elisha. Would they draw a blank? Or see part of a fireplace? What does *fast* mean to older pupils? A person observing a religious *fast* abstains from food, but someone can also eat at a *fast* food place. A *fast* race horse runs rapidly, but a horse tied *fast* is not *fast* because he is *fast!*

Bending the Nail on the Back Side

One study comparing students' abilities to recall material discovered that hearing plus seeing the information produced more than six times more retention than hearing alone.

Teaching Method Used	Recall after 3 Hours:	Recall after 3 Days:
Only Audio	70%	10%
Only Visual	72%	20%
Both Audio and Visual	85%	65%

Learning begins with reception of data by the five senses. Here is how much working knowledge people have gained through each: touch, 1 percent; taste, 1.5 percent; smell, 3.5 percent; hearing, 11 percent; and sight, 83 percent. When we use audio-visuals, we are cooperating with how the Manufacturer of minds designed them to work most efficiently.

Though showing and telling rate a B+ (94 percent), we shouldn't be content to use those two senses exclusively. Though I can lift a book with only two fingers (if it's not too thick), I have a far better grip on it with all five appendages of one hand. The more we can appeal to all five senses, the more effective will be our teaching. It's much like driving a nail through a board, then bending the nail over on the back side so it's much harder to extract.

After a class *hears* about Jesus' crucifixion, for example, and *sees* some teaching pictures, let each member *touch* to his wrist the point of a large sharpened spike (such as used by railroads). *Hearing* at the same time a sound-effects tape or record of such spikes being pounded would be unforgettable. Have each person *smell* and *taste* the bitterness of vinegar after dipping a finger into a jar of it.

Now stop and think how a lesson on Jesus' resurrection might be taught through the five senses. Then brainstorm with someone how this principle might be creatively used in your next lesson.

Judy Beckett, a teacher of children, has creatively shared how this can be done in a film and book entitled *The Two-Hour, Too-Short Sunday School* (from a Christian film distributor or Ken Anderson Films).

Sameness Isn't Always Sanctified

God must like variety, visuals, and involvement because He so often utilized them in the Scripture records of His deeds. Though He is totally consistent in His character, He is also full of surprises in His methods. Are our classes ever "business as usual" with a ho-hum routine?

It's astounding to realize that the God who could do His work better by Himself usually accomplishes it through people. Only about 4 percent of God's Bible-recorded works are done single-handledly (such as creation and the conversion of Saul of Tarsus). The rest of the time He involves people—ordinary ones like you and me.

But we shouldn't have variety and visuals just for their own sake. Selection of any teaching tool should always begin with our chosen and stated purpose. Asking these questions will help us use the best method(s):

- Will this visual help communicate the meaning of Scripture?

- Could it possibly be used more than this one time?
- Will it work well with my age group and fit my time limits?
- Is there an easier or better way to achieve my goal?

Here are some suggestions for creative variety in using easily-obtained audio or visual media to involve students in Bible learning.

Putting the Parts Together

Much teaching is like asking our pupils to work a jigsaw puzzle without allowing them to see the picture on the puzzle box lid. When told God could help his hurt finger, my two-year-old nephew insisted God was asleep. His reason: God put on His swaddling clothes and went to sleep in the barn! David had not yet connected the Christmas and Easter pieces of the Bible puzzle.

Meaning and motivation are increased greatly as pupils see how the lesson parts relate to each other as well as to past and future segments.

Acrostics like this example from Ezra could be written on a board. Place the left, vertical word first, adding the rest of the horizontal lines at the right time. (Each line summarizes one of Ezra's ten chapters in order.)

Temple Proclamation of Cyrus
Exiles Return Under Zerubbabel
Masons Lay Temple Foundation
Postponement by Samaritan Opposition
Letter to King Darius
End of Temple Construction

Work of Ezra's Return
Offerings of the Exiles
Rebellion of God's People
Keeping the Foreign Wives

Students old enough to read well can make their own acrostics with a great sense of satisfaction. Have them read a Bible portion and summarize its big ideas or events in four words or less (much like making a headline for a newspaper article). After choosing a word or phrase with the same number of letters as there are units of material, guide them to restate their titles to fit the new first letters. (Try JAWS for an acrostic summary of Jonah's four chapters.)

Barry Huddleston became so engrossed with making acrostics in his devotions that he eventually summarized the Bible with them and later published his work as *The Acrostic Bible* (Thomas Nelson and Media Ministries).

Skeleton handouts (main points listed with space for notes between) encourage notetaking. Don't wait beyond third grade to get students started on lesson notetaking. Main points may be outline words, symbols, or stick-figure drawings spaced out over a page for younger students to color. Non-artistic teachers can trace from old curriculum materials, newspapers, or the telephone yellow pages onto a stencil or spirit duplicator master. Cut-out materials can be pasted or taped onto a master sheet to duplicate on a plain-paper copier. (Hint: Make one copy; use liquid correction fluid to white-out any unwanted lines, and use this copy as the master.)

Make available or help each student make a personal notebook to keep class-time papers. Divider pages can be decorated with original drawings or pictures from magazines. Take-home papers can be pre-punched for the notebooks.

Parental cooperation, if secured, can greatly extend the value of such a binder. One West Coast pastor regularly reviewed the pictures and stories his son brought home. Turn to any picture at random from the past six months of classes, and the boy could tell the basic story (without being old enough to read).

A clothesline strung across the front of the classroom allows flannelgraph figures or teaching pictures to be continuously viewed. Hang them with spring-loaded clothespins in order of their use for a ready-made review device. Sometimes take down the hanging graphics, asking early arrivals to arrange them in order from a jumbled pile. As you rehang each, ask review questions. Other times, ask students to describe the graphics with their eyes closed. Note this example from a Bible survey course for teens (*The Old Testament Express* from Victor Books).

The Old Testament "story line"

Slides Without a Camera

Slides without a camera are possible with frosted film slides (such as Kodak Ektagraphic Write-On slides, available at most photo stores). Or mount cut pieces of matte acetate in standard slide mounts (whatever size fits your projector). Draw or write on this material with felt-tip markers, colored pencils, or ball-point pens. Dry transfer letters make excellent titles. Any typewriter can print songs, Scriptures, or outlines on write-on slides.

Slides made by students during class can be immediately projected. Frosted film is also made in rolls with perforations to make a filmstrip. A pattern sheet is provided so the hand-produced images properly fit the projector (from Starex).

Pictures clipped from magazines, newspapers, or old Sunday school curriculum provide free graphics. Sometimes bring the materials to class, and let the students choose appropriate pictures to portray a point.

Coloring book cartoons can easily be converted for the overhead projector by tracing them onto transparent plastic sheets. (Remember to ask permission of the copyright holder.) Special acetate or polyester films are made for this purpose, but cutting up dry cleaner bags or clear rolls of food wrap works well, too. They can be any size up to a maximum of ten inches square (the size of most overhead projector "stages").

Not all felt-tip pens will write on plastic (some bead like disappearing ink). Try what you have first. Water-soluble overhead pens (for example, Sanford's Vis-a-Vis brand, available at office or artists' supply stores) allow you to easily erase mistakes. But perspiration is water, too. Better are permanent pens such as laundry markers or Sanford's Sharpie brand.

Create a multi-colored visual by tracing the same cartoon with different colored pens. "Open areas" (clothes or scenery) are best colored by stripes or dots instead of solid color.

For a complete guide to making and using overhead projection visuals easily and inexpensively, consult *Dynamic Bible Teaching with Overhead Transparencies* (David C. Cook). *Mr. Overhead* is a motivational teacher-training film on the subject (Ken Anderson Films).

Teachers don't have to make all the visuals they use; students can have fun preparing them, too, on either film or paper. An opaque projector (different machine from an overhead projector) can reflect an image directly from inserted books or drawings onto a screen.

Next-Best Thing to Being There

It's ideal but not always possible to have a physical model of Bible objects (such as the Tabernacle or altars). Line drawings in Bible custom books are often too small for groups to see. Enlarge small items easily for posters, bulletin boards, or chalkboard use by first making an overhead transparency of the desired graphic (unless using an opaque projector mentioned above). Projection film can be secured for any plain-paper copier, enabling transparency making as easily as a paper copy from a book. (Caution: use only the film designated for a particular copier.) A thermal copier (such as 3-M's Thermofax) is designed to make transparencies in about four seconds (but will accept only single sheets).

Project the transparency, tracing off only part, if desired, onto a posterboard or large piece of paper. An end roll of newsprint can often be secured free or inexpensively from newspaper publishers. Use a variety of colored chalks for tracing directly onto the chalkboard. The finished size can be varied greatly by how far or close the projector is placed from the tracing surface.

A small opaque projector (Magnajector) is inexpensively available in some toy stores and useable in a dark place for enlarging. Though it only enlarges from postcard-size, larger originals can be traced in sections.

Yellow drawing or lettering can "magically" appear on a dark blue background to fascinate young or old. Demonstrate the handwriting on the wall at Belshazzar's feast with 3-M's Color Highlight Write-on Film, available in kits of film sheets and special solvent markers. White-on-black and other colors are being developed. Another trick with this film is to trace a cartoon lightly with soft (cheap) chalk onto the blue film. When projected, the chalk lines are visible only to the teacher, who simply traces over them to look like an accomplished freehand artist.

Moving Places

Bible events become "more real" as students see where the action happened. Complete sets of Bible maps are available for overhead projection (Faith Venture Visuals). With permission, maps can also be traced from books using techniques described above.

Common household objects (coins, key chains, or string) project as black silhouettes when laid on the overhead projector's horizontal stage. Sandwich sticks and beverage stirrers provide swords, arrows, airplanes, and other unique markers to lay on the overhead. Any desired shape cut from paper or cardboard projects as a silhouette. Unique hand pointers are available from Faith Venture Visuals.

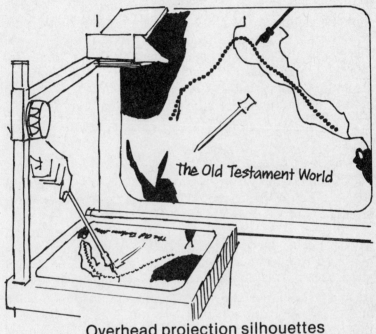

The Old Testament World

Overhead projection silhouettes

Add motion to maps (flowing lines, turning wheels, blinking titles) using Polarmotion adhesive contact material (Faith Venture Visuals). It's best to cut the desired shape before separating the backing paper, then adhere the Polarmotion film to a separate piece of plastic (not directly onto the surface of a finished visual). Motion appears as a polarized hand spinner is turned in the projected light path. It's all transparent, suitable for overhead projection.

Backgrounds, maps, and figures can be adhered instantly to walls or writing boards without glue or tape by using limp vinyl (often sold for table covers, it should feel a little tacky). Flannelgraph figures pasted to such vinyl can be superimposed on a wall map or chalkboard. Adhesion is enhanced by briskly rubbing the item to increase static electricity.

View and Review

Original pictograms make learning proper pronunciation of strange Bible words fun. Clip or crudely sketch a separate picture for each syllable of the word to be learned. For example, Capernaum might be a boy's cap + a girl (her) + a horse saying "neigh" + man thinking "um." The Dead Sea might be a coffin with a big letter "C" drawn in or on it. Some are easier, like Tyre (car tire). How many Bible books can you identify on the following graphic?

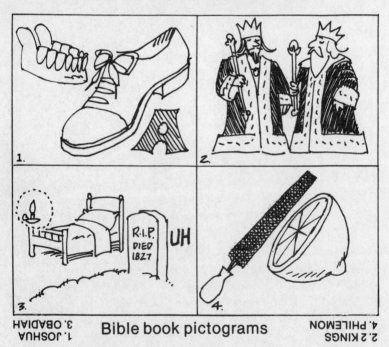

Bible book pictograms

1. JOSHUA 2. 2 KINGS 3. OBADIAH 4. PHILEMON

Make a review game of people and places from past lessons, letting the class guess them from pictures only.

Create a coat of arms for a Bible person. Draw a big shield, divided into four sections by an internal cross. Let each quadrant represent the person's background (family, parents' distinctives, or nationality), meaning of name (consult a Bible dictionary), accomplishments, or character traits. Select pictures or draw symbols as a visual summary.

Make a review banner, progressively completed through a series of lessons. For each meeting, select or create one or two symbols to recall the "big idea." After explaining the summary visual, add it to a large banner of felt or burlap displayed in your room. In later sessions, as students tell what the symbols mean, they will have grasped an overview of the whole series. The pieces could be added to a bulletin board as well or to a large flannelgraph board other than the one used in lessons (so the summary is always visually available in the room).

A mobile summary could be made by adding a cardboard symbol each session. For example, Nehemiah 1 could be summarized by a praying hands symbol, chapter 2 by a man on a horse, and 3 by a hammer and sword. Note the completed Nehemiah mobile, with which a four-year-old demonstrated his ability to grab the symbols in order and tell the idea.

Sing and Speak

If you want words big enough for a group to easily see, type them onto 35mm slides or filmstrips with any typewriter using frosted acetate instead of paper. Or hand-letter them onto a blank overhead transparency.

Be considerate of copyrights. Don't make the projectable copy to avoid buying songsheets or books for each student, and be sure you own the book from which the words are being taken.

Original newspaper ads give a unique, attention-getting twist to announcements. For an outing, for example, advertise for children with big appetites who are eager to have fun. Print the ad on a poster with some graphics or tape-record it to play as though on the radio. Add dramatics to the latter by playing some music or part of a radio program with which the people are familiar, interrupting it with an urgent announcement just received over the news wire.

"Mystery" lettering of an announcement can be made by drawing only the vertical parts of block letters. Let students guess the words as you randomly add the horizontal parts to complete the letters. Can you decipher the following lines?

Visual Assistants

Visually ask a question on the chalkboard or overhead as students arrive to whet appetites for the lesson. For example, "Who watched a worm eat a big bush?" (Jonah) Or, "Why was Job cold when he tried to sleep?" (He had miserable comforters.)

Full-color photographs for the overhead can introduce people who can't be present, such as missionaries. Copy centers in most major cities will convert any photograph or printed picture onto transparent film in a few minutes (and relatively inexpensively, too). They can also enlarge a 35mm slide to 8 1/2" x 11" film while you wait. (Consult the telephone white pages under Xerox or 3-M.)

Semi-permanent chalkboard lines and forms can be created with chalk sticks that have been soaked in a saturated sugar-and-water solution for about fifteen minutes. Information added with regular chalk is removed with an eraser, the forms only with a damp cloth.

An attendance or other recognition form can be ruled up on a transparency using a permanent marker and information added with water-soluble markers. ("Permanent" markers can be erased with rubbing alcohol if used on a good grade of plastic, acetate, polyester, or mylar.)

Ponder the next lesson you will teach. Pick out one new way to utilize a teaching tool, and plan to do it.

A carpenter doesn't *have* to use a power saw. A secretary doesn't *have* to use a computerized word processor. A housewife doesn't *have* to use a microwave oven. A teacher doesn't *have* to use audio and visual aids.

But using the best tools for the task will help you to be the best Sunday school teacher you can be.

Source Addresses

Baker Book House
Box 6287
Grand Rapids, MI 49506

Bill Hovey Visuals
5730 Duluth Street
Minneapolis, MN 55422
612-542-9970

Dale Carnegie Association
Suite 156W
6000 Dale Carnegie Drive
Houston, TX 77036

David C. Cook Publishing
    Company
850 North Grove Avenue
Elgin, IL 60120

Eastman Kodak Company
A-V Services Division
Rochester, NY 14650

Faith Venture Visuals
510 East Main Street
P. O. Box 17543
Lititz, PA 17543
800-233-3866 (outside PA)
717-626-8503 (in PA)

Ken Anderson Films
P. O. Box 618
Winona Lake, IN 46590
219-267-5774

Media Ministries
516 East Wakeman Street
Wheaton, IL 60187
312-665-4594

Moody Press
820 North La Salle Drive
Chicago, IL 60610
312-329-4000

New York International
    Bible Society
144 Tices Lane
East Brunswick, NJ 08816

Sanford Ink Company
2740 Washington Street
Bellwood, IL 60104

Starex
P. 0. Box 248
Kearny, NJ 07032

Thomas Nelson Publishers
Nelson Place at Elm Hill
      Pike
Nashville, TN 37214

3M Company
Visual Products Division
3M Center
St. Paul, MN 55101

Victor Books
1825 College Avenue
Wheaton, IL 60187

Xerox Corporation
Stamford, CT 06904

Zondervan Corporation
1415 Lake Drive, SE
Grand Rapids, MI 49506

Index

Other Books by Terry Hall

Bible Panorama (Victor)
Dynamic Bible Teaching with Overhead Transparencies (Cook)
Finally, Family Devotions That Work (Moody)
Getting More from Your Bible* (Victor)
New Testament Express* (Sonpower)
Off the Shelf and Into Yourself* (Victor)
Old Testament Express* (Sonpower)
The Projectable Bible Atlas (Faith Venture Visuals)

*Leader's guide for group study is available by same author.

Creative Teaching Seminar

A popular seminar based on the material in this book is available. Audience involvement, colorful visuals, and creative learning methods are incorporated. For more information on how your church or organization can sponsor a Creative Teaching Seminar, contact:

Media Ministries
516 East Wakeman
Wheaton, IL 60187
312-665-4594

Moody Press, a ministry of the Moody Bible Institute, is designed for education, evangelization, and edification. If we may assist you in knowing more about Christ and the Christian life, please write us without obligation: Moody Press, c/o MLM, Chicago, Illinois 60610.